Living in Hope

People Challenging Globalization

edited by

John Feffer

with a preface by

Martin Garate

ZED BOOKS
LONDON AND NEW YORK

AMERICAN FRIENDS SERVICE COMMITTEE
PHILADELPHIA

Living in Hope
was first published in 2002 by
Zed Books Ltd, 7 Cynthia Street, London N1 9JF, UK and
Room 400, 175 Fifth Avenue, New York, NY 10010, USA

US paperback edition published by
American Friends Service Committee, 1501 Cherry Street,
Philadelphia, PA 19102-1479, USA

Distributed in its cased edition in the USA exclusively by Palgrave,
a division of St Martin's Press, LLC,
175 Fifth Avenue, New York, NY 10010, USA

Cover design by Andrew Corbett
Set in 10½/13 pt Bembo by Long House, Cumbria, UK
Printed and bound in the United Kingdom by Cox & Wyman, Reading

A catalogue record for this book is available from the British Library
US CIP data is available from the Library of Congress
Canadian CIP data is available from the National Library of Canada

ISBN 1 84277 152 3 Hb (Zed Books)
ISBN 1 84277 153 1 Pb (Zed Books)
US Pb ISBN 0 910082 44 8   (AFSC)

Contents

contents

Preface

This book is a small and beautiful mosaic of success stories in a programme that AFSC regards as its most fundamental work for fostering peace and justice. The programme is called International Affairs and is carried out by Quaker International Affairs Representatives (QIARs) in a number of regions and countries and also at the UN with offices in New York and Geneva.

In many parts of the world, AFSC works like other international development organizations – building schools, providing medical assistance, distributing food aid. But AFSC's International Affairs work is different. It is focused not on building things but on building relationships.

The International Affairs work is rooted in the Quaker peace testimony, and from this deep commitment the work is done to further peace with justice. As such the International Affairs work seeks to promote communication in the interest of peace and justice, especially between people in conflict. The work of the representatives seeks to bring together adversaries across divides, helping them to find a common language to prevent violence and build peace. Humility is an essential component of the work of AFSC's international affairs representatives. The work is by nature quiet and facilitative. Another aspect of this work involves linking people and networking across levels: from the grassroots, national, regional, and international policy levels.

Today this work is shaped and challenged by a process that is economic, social, political, and cultural, a process that has become known as globalization, a transnational domination grounded in:

- Technologies that contaminate and ravage our resources;
- The penetration of the market into our politics, culture, human rights, and spirit;
- A pedagogy of oppression by gender, race, beliefs, and hierarchies;
- A reduction of our human condition to that of mere consumer.

As John Feffer aptly notes, 'globalization is a force that emphasizes material over spiritual growth, corporate ties over family ties, competition over cooperation'.

The shaping of the world has left thousands of millions in poverty; the reckless pursuit of markets has brought wars to millions more.

The success stories in this book showcase the work of the international representatives and their partners in the region who together are opening new possibilities for economic relations, respect of human rights, and a new culture where the person is at the centre.

These are seeds for new possibilities. They may look weak in comparison to Wal-Mart or the IMF but they are deeply rooted in the commitment of people in their search for a new ethic and values and sustained in their coming together to build a community.

AFSC presents these success stories because they represent the future of our world. What seems powerful today – the process of globalization – is in fact weak, because it is destroying more and more lives each year and cannot bring peace and justice to the majority of people in the world.

Most of AFSC's representatives and the people they work with throughout the world are not Quaker. But in different regions and in different circumstances, they are all working together in the spirit of the Quaker peace testimony, which considers every individual to be precious and demands that unjust structures be challenged.

Martin Garate *(Associate General Secretary/International Programs)*

Contributors

Arnie Alpert has been New Hampshire Programme Coordinator for AFSC since 1981. He is active in movements for economic justice and affordable housing, civil and worker rights, peace and disarmament. He is also a member of the 'Footlocker Eight', activists arrested when they protested against the Nike company's exploitation of workers in their factories. Prior to joining AFSC, Arnie worked with the Clamshell Alliance, which engaged in non-violent direct action to halt nuclear power plants. Arnie received his BA in Environmental Science from Wesleyan University and an MS in Community Economic Development from New Hampshire College. He has written articles and columns in newspapers, including the *Concord Monitor* and the *Union Leader,* in magazines and in the forthcoming encyclopedia, *Civil Rights in the United States*.

Helen Jenks Clarke holds a graduate degree in international affairs from the Norman Patterson School of International Affairs, Carleton University, Ottawa. She has conducted research in Indonesia, Malaysia, Thailand, and Vietnam. A long-time community activist in Canada, she is the author and editor of numerous reports and articles on social and economic policy and development cooperation. She is the author of 'Research for Empowerment in a Divided Cambodia', published in 2000 in *Researching Violent Societies*. She was Co-Field Director of the Cambodia Programme of the AFSC from 1996 to 1999, and since 1999 she has served as Quaker International Affairs Representative for Southeast Asia.

Robert Clarke holds a PhD in Anthropology and Sociology from the University of British Columbia. He has worked in the fields of human rights, labour, environment, and social and economic justice in Canada and Southeast Asia. He is the author of numerous articles and reports, most recently an edited collection, *Human Resource Development and Poverty Alleviation in APEC*. He was Co-Field Director of the Cambodia Programme of the AFSC from 1996 to 1999, and since 1999 he has served as Quaker International Affairs Representative for Southeast Asia.

John Feffer served as East Asia Quaker International Affairs Representative based in Tokyo, Japan, from 1998 to 2001. He studied arms control issues in Washington on a Scoville Fellowship. John has worked as an associate editor at the *World Policy Journal* and is co-editor of *Europe's New Nationalism* (Oxford University Press, 1996) and *State of the Union* (Westview, 1994). He is also author of *Beyond Détente* (Hill and Wang, 1990) and *Shock Waves* (South End, 1992).

Brewster Grace is currently on the staff at the Quaker United Nations Office in Geneva, Switzerland where he has written extensively on multilateral financial institutions. He worked from 1973 to 1980 as the Southeast Asia correspondent for the American Universities Field Staff, where he wrote many articles on Southeast Asian economic and political development. In 1974 and 1975 he reported on the emergence and then repression of the free trade movement in Thailand. From 1985 to 1988 he was the AUFS correspondent to the United Nations in Geneva and European Commission in Brussels and wrote on the ILO and GATT.

Ricardo Hernández is director of AFSC's Mexico–US Border Programme. He has ten years' experience in grassroots organizing and edited *The Other Side of Mexico, Alternative News and Analysis for the International Community*. During 1995–6, Ricardo launched a comprehensive project on the Interamerican Development Bank, campaigning for access to information on multilateral development banks. He has also worked with the Interhemispheric Resource Center in New Mexico, co-authoring *Cross-Border Links,* a directory of organizations in Canada, Mexico and the United States.

Karin Lee served as East Asia Quaker International Affairs Representative for AFSC based in Tokyo, Japan from 1998 to 2000, during which time she covered activities in South and North Korea, China and Japan. She has written for *Korean Quarterly, Foreign Policy in Focus* and *Peace Magazine.* Karin also worked as Associate Director of Planned Giving for AFSC after graduating from Haverford College with a degree in Chinese studies and a period of study of Mandarin in Beijing.

Njoki Njoroge Njehu, the Director of 50 Years Is Enough: US Network for Global Economic Justice, is a Kenyan national who worked with women's groups and the Greenbelt Movement in Kenya before coming to the US for college in 1986. Njoki worked as an environmental activist with Greenpeace International for three years, where she focused on the international trade in toxic wastes and on biodiversity and oceans. She joined the 50 Years Is Enough Network in July 1996 and became its Director in October 1998. She serves on the board of the Quixote Center and on the Advisory Committees of the Campaign for Labor Rights and ACERCA. She is also a member of the International Committee of the World Social Forum, the Africa Social Forum, and a volunteer in various capacities, especially fundraising, for the Inter Faith Group Kenya and Jubilee South. At the 50 Years Is Enough Network her responsibilities include media work, fundraising, and being the lead spokesperson for the Network at fora around the world.

Le Thi Hoai Phuong is currently Programme Director of Quaker Service Viet Nam and has worked with the programme since 1990. She previously worked with the Vietnam Union of Friendship Organizations from 1977 to 1990 and with the Vietnam–American Association in Haioi from 1974 to 1976. Phuong was born in Hanoi and lived there throughout the war. She studied Russian and English Language and Literature in the Hanoi College of Foreign Languages. She has also studied English at Ealing College in London, Project Management in Hanoi, Gender Studies in Thailand, and is working on her Master of Science in Administration through Andrews University in Michigan.

Mary McCann Sanchez served as AFSC's Central America Co-Field Representative from 1991 to 2000. Based in Siguatepeque, Honduras, with her husband and Central America Co-Field Representative Trinidad Sanchez, Mary was responsible for directing AFSC's grassroots programmes in health and human rights in the region. From 1996, Mary also shouldered the responsibilities of AFSC's International Affairs work in Central America, which included, among other things, work on Export Processing Zone labour issues.

James Whooley has been Regional Director for AFSC's Europe Programme since 1999 and is based in Sarajevo, Bosnia. Prior to joining AFSC, James worked in Kosovo with the Humanitarian Law Documentation Project of the International Crisis Group. He was a contributor to that project's published report, *Reality Demands: Documenting Violations of International Humanitarian Law in Kosovo 1999.* James is a graduate of Columbia University's School of International and Public Affairs and served as an associate editor at the *Journal of International Affairs.*

Abbreviations

3D	Dirty, dangerous, difficult (jobs)
AFL–CIO	American Federation of Labour– Congress of Industrial Organizations
AFSC	American Friends Service Committee
AMRC	Asia Monitor Resource Centre
ARENA	Asian Regional Exchange for New Alternatives
B & H	Bosnia-Herzegovina
CAW	Committee on Asian Women
CBD	Convention on Biological Diversity
CEO	Chief executive officer
CEPAL	Consejo Económico para America Latina
CFO	Comité Fronterizo de Obreras
CGA	Community Gardening Association
CIDECA	Consejo de Investigacions para el Desarrollo de Centroamérica
COMAL	Red de Comercialización Comunitaria Alternativa (Alternative Community Trade Network)
CORDES	Fundación para la Cooperación y el Desarrollo Comunal de El Salvador
CRIES	Coordinadora Regional de Investigaciones Económicos y Sociales
DAWN	Development Alternatives with Women for a New Era
EU	European Union
FAO	Food and Agriculture Organization
FOCUS	Focus on the Global South
FTAA	Free Trade Area of the Americas
FUNDE	Fundación Nacional para el Desarrollo
GATT	General Agreement on Tariffs and Trade
HIPC	Heavily Indebted Poor Countries Initiative
HKCIC	Hong Kong Christian Industrial Committee
HSA	Hemispheric Social Alliance
IFAT	International Federation of Alternative Trade
IFI	International financial institution
ILO	International Labour Organization
IMF	International Monetary Fund

KCTU	Korean Confederation of Trade Unions
KR	Khmer Rouge
LDC	Less-developed country
MAI	Multilateral Agreement on Investment
NAFTA	North American Free Trade Agreement
NGO	Non-government organization
NIC	Newly industrialized country
OSCE	Organization for Security and Cooperation in Europe
PARC	Pacific–Asia Resource Centre
PMB	Project Management Board
PROCOSOL	Red de Producción Orgánica y Comercialización Comunitaria
PRSP	Poverty Reduction Strategy Process
PSPD	People's Solidarity for Participatory Democracy
QIAR	Quaker International Affairs Representative
QSV	Quaker Service Vietnam
RACC	Red Argentina de Comercio Comunitario
REDCOM	Red Colombiana de Desarrollo y Comercialización Comunitaria
REDECC	Red Ecuatoriana de Comercialización Comunitaria
RELACC	Red Latinoamericana de Comercialización Comunitaria (Latin American Alternative Community Marketing Network)
REMACC	Red Maya de Comercialización Comunitaria (Mayan Network of Community Marketing)
REMECC	Red Mexicana de Comercialización Comunitaria
RENACC	Red Nacional de Comercialización Comunitaria
RENACES	National Network of Alternative Marketing in El Salvador
RENICC	Red Nicaragüense de Comercialización Comunitaria (Nicaraguan Network of Community Marketing)
RGT	Red Global de Trueque
RICAA	Red de Intercambio y Comercio Alternativo de Abya Yala
RMALC	Red Mexicana de Acción Frente al Libre Comercio
SEC	Securities and Exchange Commission
TINA	There Is No Alternative
TNC	Transnational corporation
TRIPs	Trade-Related Intellectual Property Rights
UCA	University of Central America
UN	United Nations
UNCTAD	United Nations Conference on Trade and Development
UNDP	United Nations Development Programme
UNHCR	United Nations High Commissioner for Refugees
UPOV	Union for the Protection of New Varieties of Plants
VOFA	Vidarhba Organic Farmers Association
WTO	World Trade Organization

Challenging Globalization: an Introduction[1]

John Feffer

Globalization is a Nike trainer on every foot, a Golden Arch in every town, a Madonna on every magazine cover, a sweatshop in every alley, a Coke on every table, a big dam on every river, a cloud of pollution on every landscape, and 'structural adjustment' in the speech of every government leader. Globalization is an assembly line circling the world, generating ever more 3D jobs (dirty, dangerous, difficult) and widening the gap between rich and poor. Globalization is the same answer to a multitude of problems: 'Let the market decide.' Globalization is TINA (There Is No Alternative), which Margaret Thatcher declared victorious after the collapse of communism in Eastern Europe.

On the other hand, globalization can't be all bad. After all, with globalization has come the spread of technical advances, greater intercultural contact and international solidarity. When New Yorkers eat sushi, Tokyoites dance to Hong Kong pop, Chinese watch French movies, Parisians read Senegalese novels, the residents of Dakar visit Argentinean web sites and New York-style bagels are a hit in Buenos Aires, globalization seems to have expanded our options rather than limited them. Beyond a circle of upwardly mobile urbanites, globalization has also helped to raise the visibility of international labour standards, respect for human rights, and movements for women's emancipation. Globalization brought the world leaders to Seattle for the World Trade Organization (WTO) meeting in 1999, but it also brought an international array of protesters to the Seattle streets.

Is there a 'good' globalization and a 'bad' globalization? Do we need more than one word to describe this phenomenon? Is globalization in all its forms inevitable or merely a passing fad? Are we heading toward 'one world ready or not' with no turning back, no detours, no forks or even speed bumps in the road?

In this book, we will try to address these difficult questions from various angles. While recognizing that the social and cultural implications of globalization are crucial, we will focus nevertheless on globalization as an economic force that has moved powerfully across borders. We will try to understand this aspect of globalization not just from the top of the pyramid, but from all levels – the personal, the local, the regional, the national as well as the trans-national.

Most importantly, we will tell some stories. You'll meet Juany Cázares and Paty Leyva who stood up to a US clothing manufacturer in Mexico, Tet Non who makes mosquito nets to support her family and help build a sustainable alternative in her Cambodian village, the Footlocker Eight who challenged Nike in New Hampshire, and activist and entrepreneur Safia Minney who has built up a fair trade company in Japan. These are testimonies from people around the world who have gone about things a little differently. And successfully.

This introduction places these stories in a larger context by providing some background on globalization – its history and chief defining characteristics – and also by identifying some of the themes that run through the essays in this book.

Globalization Takes Off

Globalization is nothing new. In the thousand years prior to the advent of capitalism, Asia was the centre of a global market. Arab and Indian merchants helped to create dense trade networks that crisscrossed much of the world. The Silk Road, which brought goods and information from East to West, was a kind of proto-Internet. Many of the things we take for granted today – coffee, pepper, tomatoes, silk, the printing press – were shaped by a world market that predates modern capitalism. This was a global market, to be sure, but it was not a *capitalist* market. Trade in those days was little more than barter – my silk for your gold.

As historian Immanuel Wallerstein has pointed out, the processes that we identify as globalization – the creation of a global capitalist market and an inter-state system regulated by international law – began a little over five hundred years ago.[2] Powered by the twin engines of colonialism and capitalism, globalization took on a distinctly European flavour after 1500. European nations colonized the Americas, Africa and Asia; the gold and silver of the New World, slaves from Africa and the spices of Asia all contributed to bankrolling the rise of finance and manufacturing in Europe. Asian countries, which might have challenged the emergence of a Europe-centred global capitalist market, retreated into relative isolation,[3] and the Islamic world that contributed to the intellectual underpinnings of the European renaissance fell victim to internal strife and decline.

During this period of expansion and consolidation, European countries to a greater or lesser extent became modern: building powerful capitalist economies, establishing political bureaucracies, standardizing languages and educational systems, constructing national cultures, raising new factories and new cities, revolutionizing science and technology, and inventing new weapons of destruction. Within Europe itself, the modernization process encountered many challenges – peasant revolts, Luddite machine-breaking, regional uprisings, religious opposition. And globally, European nations encountered similarly strong responses in the countries they had colonized, as slaves rebelled, nationalist movements gathered strength and pressed for independence, and anti-imperialist wars broke out. The campaign against colonialism, which began at the end of the nineteenth century, was the first international challenge to the spread of European power. These responses to the modernization process – at both the periphery and the core of the world system – find their echo today in protests against globalization by US factory workers and Thai fisherfolk alike.

By the beginning of the twentieth century, with the addition of the United States to the Euro-consensus on building a world system, a global market was in full swing, with international trade playing an increasing role in national economies. It was not until the twentieth century, however, that the global spread of the capitalist market encountered systemic, transnational opposition. The rise of communism in the Soviet Union and the emergence of fascism in Italy and Germany represented the first ideological challenges on a global scale. The fight against fascism led to the bloodletting of the Second World War; the confrontation between communism and capitalism developed into the Fifty Years War, otherwise known as the Cold War.

Although the world was divided into two blocs after the Second World War, one key economic idea bridged the gap: the drive for rapid economic growth, which lay at the heart of both capitalism and communism. Even in the Third World, an independent bloc of post-colonial countries, economic and political alternatives were premised on economic growth. As Walden Bello has pointed out, 'In the three decades after 1950, the South's rate of economic growth was not only higher than the North's during the same period, it was also higher than the rate for the developed countries in their early stages of development.'[4] In the late 1970s, however, the falling price of commodities and the rising price of oil threw much of the Third World into debt. The very notion of 'development', by which the poorer countries of the world were supposed to catch up with the industrialized North, fell into discredit.

In the last decade of the Cold War, with the communist bloc stagnant or near collapse and the dominant development model under attack, a new consensus on economic development was emerging in the conference rooms of Washington, DC. This

'Washington consensus', as it was dubbed in 1990, drew much of its inspiration from the radical free market reforms of Ronald Reagan in the US and Margaret Thatcher in the UK, though even so-called socialists such as François Mitterrand implemented similar reforms in France.

The new consensus, which drew support from bankers, economists, politicians and policy analysts, centred on the need for 'liberalization' even of reasonably healthy economies and 'structural adjustment' of the less healthy. Advocates of the Washington consensus recommended (or insisted) that governments in the developed and developing worlds alike privatize publicly owned properties; eliminate barriers to foreign investment; cut government spending and therefore government services; and introduce 'labour market flexibility' by firing full-time workers, eliminating benefits, and relying on temporary and part-time labour. For the once communist countries, the Washington consensus translated into 'shock therapy' as the old economies were liberalized virtually overnight. China and Vietnam, although they remained communist, increasingly began to follow the advice of international bankers and representatives from the International Monetary Fund (IMF) and World Bank. Even the most isolated areas of the world were not immune, as North Korea created a free trade zone in 1991 to attract foreign investment.

There have been different approaches to capitalist development, of course. Germany has emphasized a social market system in which labour participates more fully in economic decision making. Scandinavian countries similarly have created strong social welfare systems. But even these countries began to adapt to the Washington consensus during the 1990s.

Which left only one major challenge. This was the 'Asian model of development', the state-directed economic policies that brought Japan, South Korea, Taiwan and Hong Kong into the ranks of the industrialized world.[5] These countries (later joined by mainland China) were the great exceptions to the post-Second

World War rule that the rich countries got richer and the poor countries stayed relatively poorer. The *per capita* growth rate in these countries was 5 per cent per year from 1965 to 1995, at a time when the average rate for the rest of the developing world was a mere 1.5 per cent.[6] The US supported these economic heresies because strong, stable East Asian countries were necessary in the larger Cold War conflict.[7] In its early phases, this Asian model of industrialization proceeded more equitably than earlier processes in the West.[8] On the other hand, economic growth largely took place in undemocratic environments.[9]

In the 1990s, this rival approach to economic development received a double blow. The Japanese economy went into a slow decade-long tailspin after 1989 when its financial bubble burst. And in 1997, as a result of speculative capital flows, removal of key state regulations, and pervasive corruption, the Asian financial crisis broke across the region, spreading from Thailand to points north and south.[10] The IMF stepped in to provide capital as a kind of bridging loan, but the price was high. Governments in the region were expected to restructure their economies according to the familiar recipe: lowered trade barriers, privatization and the sale of assets to foreign interests. The Washington consensus, it seemed, had bested the Asian model of development. This victory may well prove temporary if stronger social market societies or government-led development or some other model of political economy becomes dominant in the future.

Defining Globalization

By the dawn of the new millennium, then, the key features of a new kind of globalization were in place. These can be identified as:

Growth – The common element of capitalism and communism remains at the core of globalization. As the saying goes, 'the rising tide lifts all boats': only through growth can countries develop.

The engine of this growth has increasingly become private enterprise. Some policy analysts have taken the argument to the next logical level and advocate a 'global Keynesianism': an economic stimulus package that would expand the world economy even more. There are four major problems with the economic growth fostered by globalization: environmental limits, persistent inequality, overproduction and debt. Even as the global GNP rises, it is unclear who will buy all the new products rolling off the assembly lines. The world's companies are currently producing more cars and clothes and toys than the world can buy. Consumption has been sustained in large part by debt: the debt of countries (whether Uganda or the United States) and the debt of consumers (primarily in the US).[11] High levels of debt cannot be sustained indefinitely. Even if all of the world's people manage to buy all of the goods being produced, with cash or on credit, can the environment absorb all the pollution that results from the factories and the exhaust pipes of the cars? Growth has also not done much to improve equity. Despite the growth of global GNP, the Northern countries that were 20 times richer than the Southern countries in 1960 were 46 times richer by 1980.[12] The situation did not improve after 1980. The world's 48 least-developed countries, with 13 per cent of world population, had a mere 0.4 per cent of exports and 0.6 per cent of imports in 1999, a decline of more than 40 per cent since 1980.[13]

Free trade – Governments have long protected their national industries from foreign competition by erecting trade barriers. These barriers usually consist of a tariff or tax placed on imported goods so that they are less likely to be bought than local products. Economic growth in the globalized world is linked to increasing trade among countries, which translates into removing all tariffs as well as 'non-tariff barriers to trade' such as certain environmental regulations and government subsidies of industry. Free trade has been promoted on a bilateral basis, regionally and internationally.

There are essentially two types of free trade agreement: removal of trade barriers between relative equals and between relative unequals. Regionally, the European Union is an example of the first, as European countries have gradually reduced internal barriers to trade among member states. The North American Free Trade Agreement, encompassing the United States, Mexico and Canada, is an unequal agreement, since the weakest partner, Mexico, can no longer use trade barriers to build up its local industry. In both cases, these regional pacts discriminate against non-members. The global agreements are similarly unbalanced. First through the General Agreement on Tariffs and Trade (GATT) and now under the auspices of the WTO, the richer countries have tried to sustain their advantage over poorer countries by reducing tariffs worldwide and guaranteeing markets for their goods. Free trade creates a bigger pie, but not everyone has access to the same desserts.

Deregulation – In addition to removing barriers to trade, national governments have dismantled a good part of the regulatory structures built up in the twentieth century. For instance, national governments have removed regulations in the banking and financial world, resulting in fiascos such as the Savings and Loan crisis in the United States and the rapid movement of capital that destabilized governments and economies in the recent Asian financial crisis. With the removal of tariffs and the lessening of controls on the flow of money, governments have fewer levers with which to control corporations and private investors. Globalization, in other words, has led to a weakening of state power and an increase in economic insecurity, particularly among medium-sized and smaller states. Markets, after all, are about risk and insecurity – the opposite of lifetime guarantees of employment as in Japan or the 'iron rice bowl' of China.[14] Whether through the market transitions in the formerly communist world or the liberalization of East Asian economies or the structural adjustments of the Third World or the austerity measures in the industrialized world, the spread of the market has meant an increase in economic insecurity. Free trade has further undermined national agreements on labour and social services that have traditionally ensured economic security and protected 'citizens from the relentlessness of the free market'.[15] As a result, deregulation removes safety nets that protect the vulnerable and the fire walls that control market activity.

TNCs and monopolies – Producing one-third of world output, transnational corporations (TNCs) control 70 per cent of world trade, 80 per cent of foreign direct investment, and 70 per cent of patents and technological transfers.[16] Deregulation has clearly benefited these corporations. Although anti-trust legislation still partitions the occasional conglomerate, corporate power has become concentrated in fewer and fewer hands. The frenzy of 'mergers and acquisitions' that began in the 1980s has created enormous transnational corporations with widespread and multifaceted interests. Some corporations, such as Microsoft and Intel, have created virtual monopolies in the fields of new technologies. Media barons such as Rupert Murdoch, Viacom and Bertelsmann have created huge empires that stretch across television, newspapers, book publishing and radio. Transnational corporations, in their quest for ever cheaper labour, have created global assembly lines where computer chips are made in one country, circuit boards in another, monitors in a third, software in a fourth, and so on. In part because of the ease with which TNCs can relocate stages of these assembly lines, it has become increasingly difficult for trade unions to organize the globalized workplace. There are few institutions that have the global reach to regulate corporations. The International Labour Organization has excellent core labour standards, but these have not been ratified in many countries; the UN office for monitoring transnational corporations was downsized and turned into a promoter of investment in 1992.

Privatization – Economic development in the industrializing world of the nineteenth century depended to a large extent on government control of key enterprises such as transportation. In the 1920s and 1930s, as a response to a global depression, political movements as different as the New Deal, Soviet communism and European fascism turned to greater state control of the economy as a way to employ people and restore productive capacity. During the Cold War, the state began to lose favour as the motor force of economic development. Beginning in the 1980s, the United States, France, Chile, Japan, New Zealand and other countries began to transfer public properties (railroads, utilities, manufacturing, government services) into the hands of private corporations. In the 1990s, the communist and formerly communist world followed suit. These 'commons' are not simply factories or train lines. They can be plants and genetic material that pharmaceutical companies control, government research that is subcontracted to private firms, or even the digitalized images that are being bought up by the Microsoft Corporation. Globalization is whittling away at the very notion of the common wealth.

Market fundamentalism – The above elements – economic growth, free trade, deregulation, privatization, and the global spread of corporate power – have been combined into a powerful ideology. According to this philosophy, the market can solve all problems. And nothing should interfere with the market, neither the government nor private organizations, neither religion nor family. Market principles of competition, risk and efficiency are raised to the level of laws. Those who question these laws are considered heretics. There is one great exception to this rule: national security. Governments continue to subsidize military production; IMF structural adjustment programmes rarely lead to reduction in military expenditure; and the 'security exception' clause in trade agreements permits countries to shield military subsidies from trade negotiations.

Technological advances – Globalization has been accelerated by major advances in both computer technology and in communications. Computers have made the standardization of national economies easier; the fax, the cellular phone, and especially the Internet have increased the speed with which companies and individuals can communicate with one another. Satellite technology has facilitated this communications revolution and made the instantaneous transmission of images possible. The Tiananmen Square protest of 1989 was the first news event covered by satellite news, which affected the very process and outcome of the event. The pace of the revolutions in Eastern Europe later that year was likewise influenced by the rapidity of communication. But here, too, a gap is emerging. Not everyone in the world has a computer or even a telephone; not everyone is connected to the Internet. Fifty per cent of South Koreans use the Internet every day compared to only 0.2 per cent of Africans.

Dependency – As the world becomes more interconnected, it also becomes more dependent. As countries come to rely on imports rather than domestic production, on communication systems that are based in other countries, on regional and international trade agreements, and on environmental accords that address international problems such as global warming, cooperation becomes a key component of an effective system. 'Singapore, the only totally urbanized nation in the world, is a city that depends entirely on the outside world for its lifeblood – water from Malaysia, landfill from Indonesia, food and other products from all over the world,' writes environmentalist Alastair Gunn. 'However, Singapore is only an extreme version of life in a globalized economy.'[17] But here, too, the stronger the country, the less dependent it is. The US continues to act unilaterally in the world. For smaller and weaker countries, meanwhile, globalization has fostered a precarious dependency.

Free market and democracy – It has become a tenet of the new globalization that there can be no free market without democracy and no democracy without the free market. According to this argument, the free market is inherently democratic by virtue of providing more choices, and democracy can only flourish where the 'rule of law' supports private property and commerce. The tensions between the market and democracy – such as the influence of money on politics or the undemocratic nature of most workplaces – are rarely explored. Moreover, the key decisions concerning economic globalization take place in rarefied places: the ministerial meetings of the WTO, the board meetings of the IMF, the staff meetings of the US Federal Reserve, the offices of investment banking firms. The very institutions calling on national governments to be more transparent have rarely opened up their own decision-making processes to outsiders (if more than 5 billion people can fairly be termed 'outsiders'). Even when key documents are available to the public, they remain inaccessible. The final document of the Uruguay Round of negotiations published in 1994 was, for instance, 22,000 pages long and weighed 385 pounds.[18]

Transparency – Related to this new consensus on the relationship between democracy and the market is the notion that the 'rule of law' is necessary for the proper functioning of the market. The rule of law permits the market to function efficiently. Problems with inefficiency are then attributed to corruption or other political failures. But as analyst Robert Kuttner points out, 'a much more plausible analysis is simply that a market system, precisely because of imperfect information, asymmetries of power, and lags in deterrent mechanisms, provides ample latitude for opportunism'.[19] Globalization, by removing restrictions on market activity, has raised this opportunism to a higher level.

One additional aspect of the new globalization deserves attention: who is pushing globalization?

It should come as no surprise that global institutions support globalization. In the wake of the Second World War, world leaders sought to create global institutions in order to manage economic relations. These institutions have grown in importance and influence in recent decades. The World Bank has become the chief supplier of funds for 'development' projects around the world; the IMF lends money to needy countries but only with certain strings attached. The United Nations, through the UN Development Programme (UNDP), has also played a large role in determining the shape of economic development. The WTO has become the centre of multilateral trade negotiations. These inter-national institutions are not subject to democratic elections; they are all disproportionately influenced by the United States (through contributions in the case of the IMF and World Bank; through withholding money in the case of the UN; and through lobbying in the case of the WTO). These institutions also tend to be shaped by prevailing economic views. While it might have praised worker self-management in Yugoslavia in the 1970s, the World Bank has increasingly relied on market instruments to encourage development. The WTO promotes free trade. The UNDP has turned to corporations to help support its operations.[20]

In addition to international institutions, the most powerful economic countries in the world have generally favoured global-ization and none more so than the United States. There have certainly been dominant powers throughout world history. China controlled much of Asia; Rome controlled Europe and parts of Africa and Asia; Spain ruled over much of the New World. But the role that the United States is playing in the new dispensation is of a different order of magnitude. As a recent study of global-ization concluded, 'globalization is not just a set of trends, but also a conscious political project'.[21] That political project has been to concentrate power in the hands of an elite group of countries, institutions and corporations – led by the United States. While deregulation has weakened the role of the state to conduct domestic policy, globalization has in fact strengthened the capacity of large states to operate internationally. Whether through the decisions of the Federal Reserve Bank (on interest rates), major US banks (on Third World debt), US investment houses (on capital flows), or US cultural institutions (on the content and distribution of films), the United States has attempted to use globalization as a method of consolidating political and economic power.

Thus, US championing of free trade has not been in support of an abstract principle but as a method of opening foreign markets to US goods. Similarly, the US supports the IMF's structural adjustment programmes not simply because of faith in certain economic principles. Thus Mickey Kantor, former US Trade Representative, has said, 'the troubles of the tiger economies offered a golden opportunity for the West to reassert its commercial interests. When countries seek help from the IMF, Europe and America should use the IMF as a battering ram to gain advantage.'[22] The same asymmetries apply to consumption. The US has not only been the pacesetter in terms of free trade and the cult of deregulation, it has also consumed the lion's share of the world's natural resources. With only 4 per cent of the world's population, the US consumes one-third of global natural resources and produces two-thirds of global waste.[23]

Globalization, then, is a set of economic policies that emphasize growth and the role of the market at the expense of the state. It is the culmination of certain trends in technology. Politically, it favours democracy and transparency, though often only in a formal sense. And it is pushed forward by international institutions and the largest economic powers, particularly the United States.

Challenging Globalization

Some of the challenges to the new globalization resemble earlier attacks against colonialism, modernization or US hegemony. But the new opposition centres around world trade in goods, services and culture. Japanese farmers don't want cheap American rice to ruin their domestic market. The French government is trying to keep English words from creeping into the French language. The Korean movie industry is fighting against the intrusions of Hollywood.

Some of the challenges are more systemic. The trade union movement has challenged many of the key components of globalization – free trade, the spread of TNCs, or the government deregulation that aids business but not labour. Trade unions are organizing at the workplace level as well as at the national, regional and international levels. The environmental movement, meanwhile, has taken issue with the concept of unimpeded growth at the heart of globalization. Green activists have opposed dam projects, deforestation and timber projects, genetically modified food, the pollution of the air and earth and sea. Green activists have joined hands with labour activists to oppose free trade agreements. And both movements have created their own forms of globalization – trade union internationals and worldwide Green organizations – but a globalization based on cooperation rather than competition.

Some of the challenges to globalization focus on specific campaigns. The Fifty Years is Enough group is fighting against the inequitable policies of the World Bank. Jubilee 2000 has laboured long and hard to cancel the crushing debt owed by the developing world to the banks and treasuries of the developed. The campaign against the Multilateral Agreement on Investment, an agreement favouring businesses and wealthy countries, successfully (though perhaps only temporarily) scuttled the proposal.

And then there are the intellectual and philosophical challenges to globalization. A diverse group of thinkers — Susan George, Vandana Shiva, Walden Bello, William Grieder, Martin Khor, John Gray – have published stinging critiques of globalization in recent years. Religious leaders and groups, from the Pope to Muslim clerics, have challenged globalization as a force that emphasizes material over spiritual growth, corporate ties over family ties, competition over cooperation. Even some of the early proponents of globalization are getting worried. George Soros, who made billions of dollars in the deregulated world of finance, began to criticize the very mechanisms that made him wealthy.[24]

These, then, are the challenges. Are there any alternatives?

In Eastern Europe after 1989, it was common to hear people talk about the need to avoid experimentation when undertaking economic reform. They equated communism with an unsuccessful experiment and wanted something that 'worked'. But the market has not worked for many people and for many places. It is perhaps this gap between the market's promise and its reality that prompted former World Bank economist Joseph Stiglitz to remark, 'New and complex situations call for experiments; not one but many experiments.'[25]

There have been many experiments, both proposed and enacted. Recognizing the toll that unregulated financial transactions have had on the developing world, economist James Tobin has recommended a tax on financial transactions that would simultaneously dampen the flow and raise money to assist countries adversely affected by globalization. Unions and non-government organizations (NGOs) have devised codes of conduct to ensure that TNCs abide by core standards in terms of wages, health and safety, and environmental regulations.[26] Communities have created 1,000 alternative currencies in Europe and North America to encourage local, sustainable economic activities.[27] Realizing that remittances from migrant workers to their families in the Philippines far exceed the level of foreign direct investment in the country (US$7 billion versus $1.1 billion in 1999), a regional NGO in Hong Kong has established a programme called Migrants Savings for Alternative Investment.[28] The savings of migrant workers are funnelled as much as possible into investments back home rather than simply into consumer goods. In a forbidding, resource-poor region of Colombia, the community of Gaviotas

pioneered so many labour-saving, energy-efficient and economi-
cally sustainable methods that it became a model for communities
around the world.[29]

Representatives of the American Friends Service Committee
(AFSC) have worked both locally and internationally to support
economic justice and greater democratic representation of the
grassroots. Part of this work has been to raise the voices of those
adversely affected by globalization, voices that are so often overlooked by media, by governments, by international organizations.
Together with partner organizations and allied groups, the AFSC
works with a wide range of people – small-scale farmers in
Honduras, migrant labour in the Andes, the urban poor in Bosnia,
Cambodian woodcutters, Mexican textile workers, Korean NGO
activists, Vietnamese government officials, Swiss bureaucrats and
many more.

Because economic globalization takes place at many levels,
these responses also have taken place at different levels, as the
following essays demonstrate. At the local level, as in the Community Gardening Project in Sarajevo, Bosnia, a multi-ethnic
group of urban farmers is growing food together in an experiment
that meets basic needs but also forges reconciliation in a divided
society. In Vietnam, credit programmes have been started in
several provinces in an attempt to serve those left out of the
government's staged transition to a market economy. A community
marketing network in Central America helps rural farmers get fair
prices for their produce. Activists on sweatshop campaigns are
working transnationally to challenge TNCs. And policy analysts
working at a multilateral level in Switzerland are seeking ways of
strengthening national campaigns to protect genetic resources and
biodiversity from corporate control.

Running through these stories are several themes.

• Many regions, countries, nations, localities, and, above all,
people have been left behind in this current remaking of the

globe. Successful challenges to globalization have met the *basic needs* of those who are not benefiting from globalization, whether in terms of food security, clean water or better health care.

- Communist and capitalist systems alike have relied on unsustainable growth with no regard for the environment or the health of future generations. Globalization, too, assumes no limits on growth. In devising alternatives, activists have placed ecology at the centre of their efforts. The improvement in people's lives must be *sustainable* or the improvement is only short-term.

- Sustainable economic development takes place in specific cultures and has therefore been *culturally appropriate*. What works in one country or region may not work in another. One size does not fit all.

- Globalization is about *linkage*. To devise credible alternatives and to learn from the experiences of others, activists have established networks of their own.

- The global economy relies on *information* – about prices, interest rates, national policies, international regulations. In setting up alternative markets, producers need their own sources of accurate information. To track the operations of transnational operations, activists need access to information. To establish national codes to protect genetic resources, policy makers need information.

- Although globalization has brought the world closer together, much of the economic development has gone forward on a divide-and-conquer basis. Workers in free trade zones are discouraged from forming unions; consumers are discouraged from forming cooperatives; even nations are discouraged from forming producer cartels. Except in the rare cases of the very wealthy, individuals cannot alone have much of an impact on economic globalization. By forming associations and encouraging *solidarity*, however, individuals aggregate their power and can make a difference.

- Successful alternatives empower people. Rather than be at the mercy of economic decisions made in faraway places, producers and consumers take greater control over their lives. If civil society requires active civic *participation*, then this empowerment at the local level is a precondition for true democracy.

- Thinking globally and acting locally is no longer sufficient. Globalization has an effect on all levels, from the family to international institutions. So therefore challenges to globalization are taking place at *all levels*.

One element draws all of the following success stories together: prosperity. That isn't to say that all of the people involved in these projects are thinking about money, or economic advancement, or the latest brand of television. The origin of the word 'prosperity' is *pro spere* – 'to hope' in Latin.

This, then, is a collection of hope.

Notes

1 The author would like to thank Mary McCann Sanchez, Robert Schaeffer and Karin Lee for their editorial suggestions.
2 For Immanuel Wallerstein's recent views on this subject, see 'Globalization or the Age of Transition? A Long-term View of the Trajectory of the World-System', *Asia Perspective*, Vol. 24, No. 2 (2000).
3 For a provocative look at Asian economic development, see André Gunder Frank, *Reorient: Global Economy in the Asian Age* (Berkeley: University of California Press, 1998).
4 Walden Bello, *Dark Victory* (Penang: Third World Network, 1994), p. 7.
5 World Bank, *The East Asian Miracle* (New York: Oxford University Press,

1993). Also Chalmers Johnson, *Japan: Who Governs? The Rise of the Developmental State* (Norton, 1995) and Alice Amsden, *Asia's Next Giant: South Korea and Late Industrialization* (New York: Oxford University Press, 1989).

6　Henry Rowen, 'The Political and Social Foundations of the Rise of East Asia: an Overview' in Henry Rowen, ed., *Behind East Asian Growth* (New York: Routledge, 1998).

7　Chalmers Johnson, *Blowback: the Costs and Consequences of American Empire* (New York: Metropolitan Books, 2000), p. 183.

8　In Korea, for instance, the Gini coefficient declined from 0.39 to 0.28. Task Force on Country Studies on Globalization, *Republic of Korea: Studies on the Social Dimensions of Globalization* (ILO, 1999), p. 6. For China, however, the market transition has been accompanied by greater economic inequality; see *China Human Development Report* (Beijing: UNDP, December 1997), p. 7.

9　Authoritarian or undemocratic governments have presided over South Korea, Taiwan, Hong Kong, Singapore, Indonesia, China and Thailand during the greater part of their economic modernization after the Second World War. Even Japan, which is considered a democratic country, can hardly be considered a paragon of democratic participation, particularly during the high growth years of the 1950s and 1960s. See Patrick Smith, *Japan: a Reinterpretation* (New York: Pantheon, 1997), p. 16: 'We pretend that Japan is an independent country, but fundamentally it is a military protectorate, as the Japanese, along with most people other than Americans, understand. For roughly twenty years after the occupation, Washington did in Japan what it did in many Third World countries during the Cold War: it covertly but actively supported the political elite it had restored in 1948. Then it invited the rest of the world to pretend along with Americans that Japan was a working democracy.'

10　This was not a surprise to some. For instance, see Lance Taylor and Ute Pieper, *Reconciling Economic Reform and Sustainable Human Development: Social Consequences of Neo-Liberalism* (UNDP, Office of Development Studies, 1996).

11　I owe this insight to Robert Schaeffer (personal communication).

12　Wolfgang Sachs, 'Introduction', *The Development Dictionary* (Zed, 1992), p. 3.

13　*Least-developed Countries 1999 Report* (UNCTAD, 1999).

14　'As [Barry] Buzan and colleagues point out, in a capitalist system, "the actors in a market are *supposed* to feel insecure", making the achievement of sustainable economic security inherently problematic.' Mark Beeson, 'States, Markets, and Economic Security in Post-Crisis East Asia,' *Asian Perspective*, Vol. 23, No. 3 (1999), p. 35.

15 Dani Rodrik, *Has Globalization Gone Too Far?* (Washington: Institute for International Economics, 1997), p. 36.

16 Samuel Kim, 'East Asia and Globalization: Challenges and Responses', *Asian Perspective*, Vol. 23, No. 4 (1999), p. 15.

17 Alastair Gunn, 'Rethinking Communities: Environmental Ethics in an Urbanized World', *Environmental Ethics* (Winter 1998), p. 346.

18 Robert Schaeffer, *Understanding Globalization* (Lanham, MD: Rowman and Littlefield Publishers, 1997), p. 192.

19 Robert Kuttner, *Everything for Sale: the Virtues and Limits of Markets* (Knopf, 1997), p. 313.

20 Joshua Karliner, 'A Perilous Partnership', Transnational Resource and Action Center, 1999 (http:www.corpwatch.org/trac/undp/ undp.html). The UNDP cancelled this programme in May 2000.

21 Joseph Camilleri, Kamal Malhotra and Majid Tehranian, *Reimagining the Future: Toward Democratic Governance* (Victoria: La Trobe University, 2000), p. xvii.

22 Mark Weisbrot, 'Globalization for Whom?' *Cornell International Law Journal*, Vol. 31, No. 3 (1998), p. 31.

23 Pamela Sparr, 'Living Simply', *Response* (December 2000).

24 George Soros, 'The Capitalist Threat', *The Atlantic* (February 1997).

25 Joseph Stiglitz, 'Whither Reform? Ten Years of the Transition', keynote address at World Bank annual Bank conference on development economics, 28–30 April 1999.

26 Janelle Diller, 'A Social Conscience in the Global Marketplace? Labour Dimensions of Codes of Conduct, Social Labelling and Investor Initiatives', *International Labour Review*, Vol. 138, No. 2 (1999).

27 Jeff Powell and Menno Salverda, 'Community Currencies: an Innovative System to Promote Economic Self-reliance', in *Beyond the Financial Crisis* (Hong Kong: ARENA, 1999).

28 Cited by Philippine National Statistics Office and published in the *Philippine Star,* 24 November 1999, p. 17. The NGO is the Asia Migrant Resource Centre, based in Hong Kong.

29 Alan Weisman, *Gaviotas: a Village to Reinvent the World* (White River Junction, VT: Chelsea Green Publishing Company, 1998).

Resources for Resistance

Robert Clarke & Helen Jenks Clarke

Helicopters buzzed overhead. Occasionally, one landed and armed 'forest rangers' jumped out to confiscate logs and lumbering equipment. A ban on illegal woodcutting was being enforced in Sre Ambel.

Sre Ambel is in southwest Cambodia. The district's wealth lies in its forests. Recently, the villages have swelled with migrants arriving to harvest the timber and to 'make money'. Unrestricted cutting of Cambodian timber had been illegal since 1996, but enforcement was essentially non-existent. The villagers of Sre Ambel could earn income by selling logs to neighbouring countries and to Phnom Penh for charcoal. In past years, helicopters had clattered over, carrying government troops looking for the straggling remnants of the Khmer Rouge.

But in January 1999 the helicopters flying above were looking for woodcutters and illegal sawmills. The migrants – who had come to Sre Ambel because they had lost their land elsewhere in Cambodia – had a dilemma: how could they make their livelihoods now? Their quest for cash – for land rental, rice, and basic health care – was desperate. Only a few could hope to take up work in foreign-owned factories in Phnom Penh at impossibly low wages, or to traffic their virgin daughters to Thailand and Malaysia. Should they pack up and migrate to Sihanoukville to labour on the docks of Cambodia's only port for (legitimate) shipping?

The quandary of the villagers of Sre Ambel is repeated across Cambodia and, indeed, in many villages all over Southeast Asia. How can they make a living when land is being lost to the forces of globalization? Multinational forest concessionaires can ignore the logging regulations because they can afford to bribe officials of the Department of Forestry and Wildlife. And Cambodian peasants have neither the protection of a land law nor the confidence needed to defy multinational companies coming in to grab land for industrial agriculture. The ordinary people of the region are increasingly coming under the sway of the cash economy, yet their economies remain vulnerable, and the weaknesses are evident even at the village level.

Do they have any viable choices, when factory or port jobs are hard to get, or when they cannot face selling their daughters into prostitution? Even as the pressures of a globalizing economy are changing their entire way of life, the villagers of Sre Ambel and elsewhere are finding that they do have some choices. Most of the choices entail making changes in their lives, but these changes can be for the better. By resisting, cooperating with one another and looking for alternatives, the villagers can help to ensure sustainable livelihoods for themselves and future generations.

Exposed Economies

The forces of economic and social globalization over the last decade have buffeted Southeast Asia dramatically. In the 1980s early part of the 1990s, commentators pointed to the region as a case study of globalization's success. Countries in the region were transformed, first by multinational companies engaged in resource extraction, manufacturing and assembly, and then by the arrival of large amounts of global financial capital. Business and government elites spoke with pride of their 'miracle' economies and counted the days when ever more countries in the region would be admitted to the club of the NICs (the newly industrialized countries) or, as they are referred to regionally, the 'tigers'. The regional costs of globalization were clearly visible in depleted natural resources, exploited workers, crumbling social and physical infrastructure and increasing social and political unrest. But for most members of the elite, who were immune to these costs, the picture seemed a positive one.

In 1997 the financial crisis hit the region and suddenly international capital vanished, debts grew precipitously, local currencies dropped in value, unemployment skyrocketed and millions dropped below the poverty line. When asked for help, international financial institutions (IFIs) placed stringent conditions – requiring cuts in social welfare benefits – on financial bail-outs for the worst-hit countries, Indonesia and Thailand. In some countries, governments are responding with efforts to restart the miracle by cost-cutting measures and privatization, while in others they look inward to investment controls. As a result of the crisis and the IFI prescriptions, Southeast Asians now are very well aware of the problems associated with globalization.

Cambodia, meanwhile, has been bypassed by much of the financial and economic turmoil that has struck other countries in Southeast Asia in the last two years. Ravaged by thirty years of war and the accompanying international and regional isolation, it participated in neither the dramatic regional growth of the 1980s and early 1990s, nor the dramatic collapse of the late 1990s.[1] As one of the poorest countries of the region, with an economy dependent upon international aid, Cambodia has been preoccupied with ending the domestic conflict, beginning social and economic reconstruction, and breaking through the international isolation and its role as a pawn in the international geopolitics of the region.

Cambodians have experienced a variety of horrific events in the last 30 years – five years of civil war, four years of violent revolution with the death by starvation, overwork and execution of one-fifth of the population, ten years of occupation and, until 1998, low-grade guerrilla war. Some who survived the genocidal Pol Pot regime were able to escape to the Thai border camps and avoid the hardships of the Vietnamese occupation; a few returned to, or remained in, their communities and survived quietly while keeping out of harm's way. But, for most, these were wrenching, life-transforming events. The experiences of war and violence have contributed to the movement of peoples within the country and to their continuing feelings of distrust and disorientation.

The impact of almost four years under Pol Pot left the country with badly depleted resources and a population that continues to bear the scars of years of forced labour and war. For almost twenty years after the liberation of Phnom Penh by Vietnamese forces, the war dragged on as factions of the outlawed Khmer Rouge continued to fight until their collapse in 1998, after the death of Pol Pot. The constant need to keep the country on a war footing diverted resources to a large military sector and to arms, providing an unreceptive climate for foreign capital investment. To the degree that resources were available they have been directed to rebuilding the country's war-torn infrastructure and to regaining the confidence of the international donor community in order to ensure the continued flow of aid.

Still, the influences of globalization have been felt subtly. International donors and the lender community encourage free-market initiatives and support relentless efforts to shrink the public sector and privatize public services. 'Experts' from these same organizations often attribute the failure of social and economic justice in Cambodia to the Communist Party origin of the ruling Cambodian People's Party (CPP). But the CPP has not been communist for ten years. The economy is relentlessly 'free market'. Political instability, lack of adequate legislation – for business, investment, land and natural resources, and labour – and lagging human resource development are the obstacles to overcome before Cambodia is ready to join the new global economy. Except for land (which essentially is privatized through the granting of concessions to multinational companies, with no consideration of the rights of local communities), most other state-owned capital has long been sold off, although the proceeds rarely return to the Treasury. 'Sustainable economic growth' is not in Cambodia's lexicon.

A small number of international manufacturers have tentatively established businesses in the garment and electronic component industries, but the major Cambodian products traded in global markets (aside from gems and some agricultural and fish products) are in illegal sectors: trafficking in women and children, timber, drugs and small arms.

In 1998, the World Bank estimated that Cambodia would lose its commercially valuable forests in five years to foreign timber companies from Thailand, Vietnam, Malaysia and countries in the North.

> Cambodia's forests could be commercially exhausted by 2003. The immediate and dangerous legacy ... is that timber-processing capacity in Cambodia is 2.5 million cubic meters per year, five times the maximum sustainable yield of the forests: 500,000 cubic meters.[2]

The government instituted and started to enforce a ban on uncontrolled forestry. The logging ban and subsequent (selective) enforcement have resulted solely from pressure exerted by the World Bank, the IMF and the Asian Development Bank (ADB), with their insistence on sustainable yields and the culling of revenues from such yields. Only recently has the Ministry of Finance been able to demonstrate that some revenues are coming into the Treasury.

More than 80 per cent of Cambodians live in rural agricultural villages where they gain their livelihoods from agriculture and fishing. Today these villagers are struggling to rebuild their lives without many of the traditional supports found elsewhere in the region. Villagers are beginning to face the challenge of the increasing globalization of the Cambodian economy and society, but few have the resources (either physical or social) on which to fashion resistance to the process. Desperately poor and with little education they are forced by circumstances to live with what they have.

Yet, Cambodian villagers are increasing their capacity to access local resources that may help them to resist the pull of the cash economy, a pull that would link them further to the global system. Commercial logging is the tentacle of the cash economy that is slowly reaching into these communities. If villagers can find a way to make the use of their land and resources sustainable, then they can resist the call to take up destructive – and illegal – logging or to migrate to the cities to work in factories or the informal economy of the slums. With these strategies they may be able to resist some of the forces of globalization that are swirling around them. While the situation in Cambodia is in some respects unique, the case shows how people can organize resistance at the local level. ✳

Villagers' Resources at Risk: Sre Ambel District, Koh Kong Province

Sre Ambel district is located in southeastern Koh Kong province.[3] The Khmer Rouge (KR) controlled the area until 1996 and families known as KR defectors continue to live there. Ecologically it is comprised of tropical rain forests, higher-altitude pine forests, inundated lowland forests, mangroves, rice fields, streams, coastline and islands.

The district is rich in natural resources. Its upland forests are virtually the sole source of cut firewood and charcoal – used in cooking – for the capital city (150 km away) and surrounding areas. Numerous small pick-up trucks, cars, and wagons (*remorques*), with all available space filled to overflowing, ply the road north to Phnom Penh from Sre Ambel where these products are produced. The middlemen are small-scale operators. Sawn timber, whole logs and charcoal are also exported to Thailand and Malaysia. Forests provide wood and livelihoods to many of Sre Ambel's people; however deforestation is occurring at such a rapid rate that it endangers not only the livelihoods of woodcutters but also the agricultural and marine-based livelihoods of the district. Soil erosion (aggravated by large-scale commercial cutting of forest concessions) is the major reason that farmers using slash-and-burn techniques in the upland forests abandon their farms after only two or three seasons. The district's major river is already silted to the point that large boats find it difficult to reach the town, located only seven kilometres from the sea.

Large tracts of secondary-growth mangrove forests (large trees have already been cut) are important habitats in the life cycles of many commercial fish species. A number of large rivers empty into the sea and maintenance of the mangrove forests is essential to the offshore and the inshore fisheries and to the integrity of the coast-line.

Fish catches are decreasing. While waterbirds and wildlife rarely seen in other parts of Cambodia are still found in Sre Ambel, the sale and export of many of these species to collectors and zoos are rapidly depleting the country's biodiversity.

Government statistics indicate that in 1997 the province of Koh Kong had Cambodia's highest percentage of population increase . The continuous lines of oxcarts heading south into the district for weeks during the cutting season suggest that the number of migrants is very large.

People living outside of the district town are poor and isolated. Few people are literate and the incidence of tuberculosis, malaria, and cholera is high. Some are fishers while others make their living from small lowland farms or from small forest plots. Most of these long-term residents combine some woodcutting with their other activities. Recent immigrants, who often do not have access to farmland, are almost totally dependent upon woodcutting.

Thousands of families of both migrants and long-term residents supplement their farming incomes or make their total living by cutting wood directly from the province's forests. The wood is sold in the form of whole logs, sawn timber, firewood, charcoal and poles. The best quality produce goes into the international timber trade through Thailand and Malaysia to meet the increasing demand for tropical hardwood from customers in Japan, Europe and North America.

At the local level, woodcutters who own oxen or cattle go to the forest and cut one big tree at a time. It is dangerous work: it may take several days' walk to reach a suitable tree and then it may take several days to cut the tree. The woodcutters must sleep in the forest, where they encounter wild animals, snakes and leeches. Malaria is the most common illness of men who go to the forest to cut wood. The logs are very heavy, and the loggers work with limited equipment and no safety protection. Woodcutters have many accidents, resulting in death or permanent disability. A woodcutter's draft animals also suffer from the heavy work. The animals become injured or sick and usually can work for only one or two years. During the entire process of cutting and extraction from the forest, woodcutters are subject to the hazards of military or police enforcing the logging ban or appropriating the logs for their own profit.

Once a log is cut it takes seven to ten days to bring it out of the mountains and to the sawmill or road where it can be sold. For at least two weeks of labour a woodcutter earns only five US dollars per log. Logs of lesser quality are cut into small pieces, usually by women and children, and packaged for sale as firewood. Income from this type of logging is not particularly lucrative, but it appeals to those who have no other options. Woodcutters say that if they could find alternative work they would not take up this high-risk occupation.

At the moment the forest is still healthy. A healthy natural forest lives for thousands of years. If people cut only the mature trees and leave younger trees, cutting the forest can continue to produce wood (and incomes). But if the young trees are also cut, if the land is burned or cleared of forest, their forest dies. In order to eat, woodcutting families are increasingly forced to rely on cutting younger trees to make firewood and charcoal. As these younger trees are cut, there is less and less chance for the forest to continue growing to produce more wood for the future.

The problem facing these villagers has been how to increase their incomes while avoiding practices that will so degrade their natural capital that the productive system will become unsustainable. Responding to this challenge requires a number of strategies: first, villagers need to protect their current investments in livestock, land, forests and farms; they need to learn new technologies that are more productive; and they need to learn how to make more sustainable use of existing resources. Their strategies include traditional knowledge and techniques, innovative technologies and new forms of social organization. Taken together, these approaches will provide viable alternatives for the villagers as they confront the new demands of making a living in an increasingly globalized environment.

Villagers Developing Resources for Resistance

Villagers in Sre Ambel face an initial challenge of determining their goals and planning for the changes they want. As a result of the years of war and life under totalitarian systems, villagers have had little experience in collectively identifying problems and organizing themselves to address them. There are few social institutions that bring people together, and social relations are organized along patron–client lines with the more powerful people commanding the support of the less powerful.

Working together with AFSC project staff, villagers have identified their needs and then experimented with ways to meet these needs. Initially, groups of 60–100 villagers were organized around specific problems that they had identified as important. The leaders of these large groups did not know the members well and it was difficult to foster good communication. The villagers realized that the groups needed to be smaller, and 'neighbourhood groups' made up of a small number of families have formed. They create rules and expectations for their group and choose leaders. They identify common problems, analyze and prioritize them, and then plan and undertake action to address the problems they have identified. At the conclusion of the action they collectively evaluate their work. Women in three villages have chosen to formulate small women-only groups. They select an individual who serves as the communications link with others.

In 1999, nine villages in the district organized some 40 neighbourhood groups and five women's groups. AFSC provided technical assistance for a number of activities, including 101 training days in nine different villages. Subjects included agriculture, natural resource management and health. Thirty to forty people attended each training, exposing participants to a variety of new techniques and methodologies.

Activities undertaken by these groups have included: open well construction; pig, chicken and duck raising; home garden development; soil improvement; upland farm planning and improvement; a rice lending scheme; handicraft production; and integrated pest-management activities. We will describe villagers' efforts in some of these activities below.

Malaria prevention campaign

Tet Non, age 23, is proud to have her own small business that provides income for her necessities and those of her children. She belongs to a group of women who manufacture mosquito nets in this malaria-ridden part of the country. The women claim that their small income allows them to improve their homes and keep their children in school. Net manufacturing has allowed Tet Non to set up a small store to sell fish sauce and spices to her neighbours.

Sickness in the district limits the ability of many people to earn their livelihoods. Villagers have identified malaria as one of the main obstacles. It means lost days from work on their farms and added expenses for treatment. Working with the villagers, AFSC

staff helped to design an educational campaign about malaria prevention and also a programme to make mosquito nets more
widely available in the district. Several village women have taken
up the manufacture of the nets, which are sold to their neighbours.
Every year villagers are urged to bring in the nets for 'redipping'
in mosquito-repellent chemicals. Households that can show that
they have taken action to prevent the disease receive a 'Sleep
Every Night in a Mosquito Net' T-shirt. Villagers enjoy seeing
who receives the prizes, and some comment that if they'd known
about the T-shirts they'd have listened more carefully to the educational programmes.

Villagers claim that owning a mosquito net has changed their
lives. It appears they are using the nets nightly and no one has
reported a net being used for fishing or being sold outside of the
village. Other villages in the district are now requesting a
'mosquito net day' so that they can learn to replicate the experience of their neighbours.

Forest management

Villagers are coming to realize that the natural resources on which
their livelihoods are based are coming under threat from many
sources. Increasingly they are learning new skills for the management of these resources and realizing that management by the
community will help to protect their families' future. They are
building the groundwork to develop their own people's organizations to take charge of forest management on behalf of their
communities. As these new local organizations develop they can
call on technical assistance from AFSC. They hope some day to
make formal agreements with the Cambodian government to
manage their own forests in the future.

In addition, local farmers and migrant woodcutters are making
small-scale, sustainable, upland (that is, rain-fed with no regular
supply of water) agro-forestry farms on small one-hectare lots.
Our natural resource specialist and Cambodian counterpart

conducted training sessions with frequent visits to farm plots, encouraging the farmers to plant for diversity. The farms include trees and a variety of crops to allow the family to earn money all year round. As these farms are developed, the families learn to conserve water and keep the soil on their farm fertile so that they will never need to move to a new farm. More than 850 families in several villages have participated.

Sre Ambel is also a major source of charcoal for the capital of Phnom Penh and its population of one million people. The growing numbers of poor people in the city increase the demand for charcoal, resulting in increased cutting in the forests of the district, denuding the land and causing greater erosion. Twenty-two women joined a scheme to develop half-hectare tree farms of species appropriate for charcoal production. These species grow quickly on denuded land and are appropriate for charcoal production. The women themselves experimented with various treatments to speed the germination of the seeds of this particular species of 'charcoal' tree. AFSC provided the initial seed or nursery stock and continues to encourage the group with ongoing technical assistance.

Farmers are now carrying out further trials and experiments on their own lands involving raising fish in ponds, canals and rice fields. They are developing techniques for reproducing native trees, particularly those species with potential for soil improvement and charcoal production. They have been growing orna-mental species for the cut-flower market and solving particular pest problems related to local rice and vegetable production.

Village veterinarians

Draft animals are subject to a variety of diseases, which means that they are not available for work for many days during the year. When these diseases are fatal, the farmer loses his or her invest-ment. Farmers have come together to choose one person in each village to acquire the basic knowledge to treat common diseases, to become a village vet. In twelve villages, such vets are now able to recognize and treat common diseases in cattle, buffalo, pigs and fowl. In addition, the vets participate in the newly introduced vaccination campaigns to protect animals against the major fatal diseases prevalent in the area.

In one village, farmers told project staff that in the year before the project began they lost 33 buffaloes to haemorrhagic septicemia. Now that the village vets can offer the twice-yearly vaccinations needed, over the past two years no buffaloes or cattle have been lost. Keeping their draft animals healthy has made a big difference to the livelihoods of the farmers and their families.

Adult literacy

Cambodians, particularly women, have a problem: 62.9 per cent of adults are basically illiterate, more than half of whom are completely illiterate.[4] Many villages in Sre Ambel district have no school. AFSC staff have trained volunteers intensively to carry out an adult literacy programme in their home villages. Occasionally the programme provides continuing education sessions to the more advanced volunteers. Providing rice to women as they pass the exams at the end of each module has increased the popularity of the literacy programme among women. 'If it were not for the rice, my husband would never allow me to be away from the house in the evenings', says one participant. 'I am also happy that he takes care of his children while I attend class. Now he knows that staying at home is not easy work.'

Co-management of fisheries

Kompong Som Bay is one of Cambodia's most important saltwater fishing grounds. The competition within the fishing community in this southwestern province is intense. As one fisherman explained during a workshop,

> In 1983, the government forced us to relocate (because their previous village was deemed more suited to attract foreign investors and

tourism). We were allotted small plots of rock on which to build our houses. We were told we were now to be a 'fishing village'. But in 1987 the government passed a fishing law, which does not allow us to fish in the shallow waters of the bay. Of course we break the law. We have no rice fields, we have no soil for gardens, we have no forests, and we are far from the city. What can we do, but fish? If I obey the law my children will die.

In an attempt to help the poor and the not-so-poor to work together to save the bay's sea grass beds, coral reefs, mangrove forests and breeding grounds, AFSC helped to organize a two-day 'stakeholders' workshop' to which representatives of fishers, government officials and government technical persons were invited. One of the objectives of the workshop was to introduce the idea of 'co-management for fisheries'. Using experiences gained in the sustainable forestry work described above, workshop participants were challenged to think about how the fishing community could work with the Department of Fisheries to manage the livelihood on which they depend.

AFSC staff member Ouk Ly Khim asked fishers who had 'tried out' a system of co-management to tell the workshop participants what the new programme has done. He was expecting them to talk about the 150 per cent increase in cockle yields, or the 50 per cent increase in fish catch. But the man who stood up said,

> Before we had maybe ten rich people in our community, and 600 families that did not have enough to eat. Now we are all equal – all 600 other families can eat. Our whole community is better off because we share more equally.

The villagers are making these adjustments to their lives in a changing political and economic context. The social and administrative system of the area remains unstable. Wealthy outsiders continue to speculate in lands the villagers thought they controlled and the villagers' tenure remains uncertain in the absence of a comprehensive national land law. Powerful people continue to use threats and violence to force villagers off lands now wanted for agro-industrial estates or commercial logging. As Cambodia industrializes, the imagined opportunities of city life continue to beckon.

Conclusion

The full impact of globalization has yet to hit Sre Ambel, a small isolated rural district in southern Cambodia, but the villagers have felt some of it. Villagers are learning that they can make choices and pursue livelihoods in more efficient, effective and sustainable ways and that cooperation and trust amongst themselves is helpful. This knowledge may make their resistance to these global trends more effective.

Notes

1 Intense factional fighting between the armies of the two ruling parties of Cambodia coincided with the collapse of the Thai Baht, resulting in the withdrawal of international investors and some aid programmes. At this writing, almost two years after democratic elections and the formation of a new coalition government, most of the investment and aid programmes have been reinstated.

2 Global Witness, 'The Untouchables: Forest Crimes and the Concessionaires – Can Cambodia Afford to Keep Them?', briefing paper (December 1999).

3 The district has recently been divided into two, but for the purposes of the discussion here we will maintain the original single name.

4 *Cambodia Development Review* (June 2000), published by the Cambodia Development Resource Institute.

Bringing Globalization Home
Is No Sweat

Arnie Alpert

When a small group of labour and religious activists attempted to distribute anti-sweatshop leaflets outside a sneaker store at a New Hampshire shopping mall in 1998, they expected to get public attention and arrest records. They had no idea that the 'Footlocker Eight' would soon become a household name across the state.

In most ways it was a typical Saturday at the Mall of New Hampshire, the major shopping centre in Manchester, New Hampshire's largest city. A new J. C. Penney store was opening, and Penney workers were passing out promotional flyers by the mall doorways. Shoppers, some pushing baby strollers, bustled along the wide corridors, stopping now and then to chat with each other or rest on benches at the centre of each corridor. Manchester police eyed shoppers suspiciously, trying to identify the anti-sweatshop activists, who had already notified authorities and the news media of their plans to leaflet.

Nearly thirty activists entered the mall from several entrances in groups of two or three, and blended in with shoppers. Most of them carried light blue leaflets, concealed inside folders or handbags, which described sweatshop conditions in factories that produced goods for US multinational corporations Nike, Disney, and J. C. Penney. While a few activists headed for J. C. Penney to try to talk to the manager, the rest converged on the Disney Store and Foot Locker, a retail chain which serves as Nike's biggest wholesale customer and which had been targeted for protests taking place that day in 70 cities in 6 countries.

While taking care not to interfere with people going in and out of stores, the activists began offering leaflets to shoppers. Within moments, they were approached by Mall security workers and told to stop leafleting. Most of the activists complied, but eight insisted that they had a constitutional right to pass out leaflets. The police on the scene disagreed and threatened the eight with arrest if they refused to leave the Mall. When the eight activists said they would stick by their plans to leaflet, the police gave citations to two and trucked six to the police station on charges of criminal trespass, a misdemeanour. Reporters from a local radio station and a major daily newspaper were on the scene, and news of the arrests of the anti-sweatshop activists was well known by the next day.

Within a few days, the activists' cause – the abolition of sweatshop labour and the right to free speech inside privately owned shopping malls – won the support of editorial writers at several local and statewide papers. Within weeks, coverage of the case brought additional opportunities to speak to high school and college classes, church and union groups, radio talk shows on mainstream stations, and community cable TV shows. Months later, with the legal case dragging on in the court system, the case of the Footlocker Eight, the challenge of the sweatshop and the role of the shopping mall continued to inspire local discussion, debate, and even song.

Taking on Disney

Perhaps more than any other issue associated with globalization, sweatshop production of mass consumer items, especially clothing and footwear, has awakened a mass movement of youth, religious and labour activists. Internationally, activists have used diverse tactics to draw public attention to child labour, starvation wages, excessive working hours, unhealthy workplace conditions and the suppression of workers' rights in factories that produce goods carrying labels such as Nike and Disney.

Take the example of clothing production in Haiti. According

to a 1996 report from the National Labour Committee, a New York-based group, women working at clothing assembly plants in Port-au-Prince were sewing garments for the Walt Disney Corporation for as little as 28 cents an hour, far too little to live on. Workers who protested or even attempted to negotiate with management for better conditions had been fired. It was a stark contrast with Disney's wholesome image, carried on children's clothes and toys advertising the new version of *101 Dalmatians*, which had just been released.

'During filming, the dogs who starred in Disney's *101 Dalmatians* were very well taken care of. They stayed in small dog motels, had round-the-clock care, and had personal trainers,' the fast-food chain McDonald's assured customers in its publicity for Disney toys, given out as premiums at their restaurants. In a statement with more truth than they intended, Disney's own press kit asserted, 'Our animals were treated better than most humans … in the world.'[1]

The National Labour Committee called for a week of action to pressure Disney to improve working conditions in its subcontractors' plants. The New Hampshire (NH) Programme of the American Friends Service Committee (AFSC) decided to participate.

The sweatshop problem was not only a way to raise awareness about the impact of globalization on workers, but it also gave local activists an organizing 'handle' on a complex issue. It was a way to connect globalization to de-industrialized cities like Manchester and to the stores in the malls selling clothing made in low-wage countries.

At home in New Hampshire, cities like Manchester which once had provided tens of thousands of jobs for textile and shoe workers had long been abandoned by employers searching for cheap, non-union labour. Thousands of square feet of industrial buildings still stood empty along the Merrimack River. Prime commercial real estate in downtown Manchester also stood empty, or was occupied by video parlours, second-hand bookstores and other shops typical of depressed city centres.

Intown Manchester, a community organization dedicated to reviving the downtown, reported in 1993:

> As with most cities throughout the country, central Manchester has experienced an out-migration of retail from the central city area to the suburbs. The completion of the Mall of New Hampshire was a significant event that exacerbated this trend. Existing retail and restaurant establishments in Intown Manchester primarily service the business community. There is little activity after 5 pm.

Will Thomas, a social studies teacher, recalled how busy the downtown stores were when he was a child and would accompany his mill-worker mother on paydays: 'For all intents and purposes the downtown area is a dead area.' The Mall was where the people were, and the products sold there came from far away.

The Disney Store, at the Mall of New Hampshire in Manchester, was an ideal place to reach people and send a message to the company. The leaflets stated: 'Disney clothing is made in sweatshops all over the world where workers are mistreated, denied decent wages, and fired when they unionize.' Readers were urged to write, call, or fax Disney's CEO, Michael Eisner, and urge the company to cease production in Burma and to stop using child labour in Thailand. In the case of Haiti, it called on Disney to 'see that its Haitian subcontractors raise the pay of their workers, re-hire workers who were fired for union activity or talking to human rights activists, negotiate in good faith with unionized workers, and agree to independent monitoring.'

There was just one problem: the Mall of New Hampshire is private property. Although it functions as a meeting place, cultural centre, and even an occasional sponsor of political events, its owners do not allow free exercise of speech. When two activists showed up outside the Disney Store on 9 December 1996, they were quickly met by members of the Mall's private security force and ordered to stop or be arrested.

Mall owners want to control what goes on inside their property as much as possible, to create what the Mall of New Hampshire's general manager called 'a pleasant shopping environment'.[2] Upon consultation with the New Hampshire Civil Liberties Union, however, AFSC learned that the ability of mall managers to prohibit free speech had been challenged successfully in other states. Alaska's Supreme Court had observed:

> One need only look out the window into the City of Anchorage to see the importance shopping malls play in daily life. Every day the community engages in commercial, social, political and entertainment activities in these large shopping malls, not in a central village square.

The Court ruled that 'to permit malls to stifle the reasonable exercise of speech would be to hamstring the rights established by the Alaska Constitution'.

The New Jersey Supreme Court agreed. In a case brought by peace activists during the Persian Gulf War, the Court ruled:

> We do not interfere lightly with private property rights, but when they are exercised, as in this case, in a way that drastically curtails the right of freedom of speech in order to avoid a relatively minimal interference with private property, the latter must yield to the former.

Although New Hampshire had no such precedent, the NH AFSC decided to try again to distribute leaflets about the exploitation of workers who make products sold in the Mall's retail stores, and to test the Mall's ability to restrict their free speech. The right moment came on 18 April 1998, when the Campaign for Labour Rights called for an international mobilization focused on Nike, which was already the poster company for sweatshops.

The Trouble with Nike

From its base in Beaverton, Oregon, Nike had always out-sourced most of its footwear production to Asia, beginning in

Japan. As Japanese labour costs rose in the 1970s, Nike shifted production to Korea and Taiwan, which together accounted for nearly 90 per cent of its footwear production by 1980. The company began producing in China in 1981, and also built factories in Malaysia and Ireland.[3]

Nike did produce in the US: in 1974 it opened a factory in Exeter, New Hampshire, a former shoe mill town. Another plant followed in Saco, Maine, also an old mill town. By 1977, 200 people were making Nikes at the New Hampshire plant, which as Exeter Boot and Shoe had in 1910 employed 700 workers. But, according to J. B. Strasser and Laurie Becklund in a book about Nike, 'It was hard to make shoes in America.' Labour costs were nearly US$4 an hour higher than for imports. Moreover, 'there were laws in America about what types of materials could be used. Employees had vacations, regular breaks, and weekends off.'[4]

By late 1984, Taiwanese and Korean workers were costing the company $1.10 an hour, compared to compensation costs of $8 to $11 an hour in Saco. 'The last straw for Saco,' according to Strasser and Becklund, 'was a rush of workers' compensation claims for injuries allegedly caused by the repetitive nature of the tasks.' Both US plants were closed by 1985. Thereafter, Nike's footwear would be entirely Asian in origin.

In Nike's Asian factories, workers had no access to workers' compensation insurance, vacations and weekends off. But as Asians gained power in politics and in the workplace, Nike's practice fled to less democratic locations. In a research report prepared in the late 1990s by a securities firm, analysts reported:

> If we delve deeper into where Nike has produced sneakers and its comments about political stability, we notice that Nike tends to favour strong governments. For example, Nike was a major producer in both Korea and Taiwan when these countries were largely under military rule. It currently favours China, where the communists and only two men have led the country since 1949, and Indonesia where President Suharto has been in charge since 1967. The communist party is still

very much alive in Vietnam. Likewise, Nike never did move into the Philippines in a big way in the 1980s, a period when democracy there flourished. Thailand's democracy movement of 1992 also corresponded to Nike's downgrading of production in that country.[5]

Ironically, in the fall of 1997 Nike publicists distributed packets that included this report while trying to contain damage caused by US demonstrations.

Nike workers were not passive. Ten thousand went on strike over low pay in Indonesia in 1997 when Nike contractor PT Hardava Aneka Shoes refused to comply with an increase in the minimum wage, then tried to trade the raise in base pay for a cut in the attendance bonus. Smaller walk-outs took place in Vietnamese factories producing for Nike.[6]

In the summer of 1997 the *Wall Street Journal* reported that 'Nike is perhaps the most visible company to find itself in a jam over the conditions of foreign contract factories'.[7] To defend itself, Nike sent long-time civil rights activist and former UN Ambassador Andrew Young to visit its contractor factories in Indonesia, China and Vietnam. Young found 'no evidence or pattern of widespread or systematic abuse or mistreatment of workers'. He said, 'The twelve NIKE factories that I visited in Vietnam, Indonesia and China were physically as clean and modern as any manufacturing sites I have seen in the USA and certainly did not appear to be what most Americans would call sweatshops.' Young's report said the concept of workers' rights 'is not a well-developed or well-understood principle' in the three countries. He acknowledged he had not looked into the issue of wages and living standards at all.[8]

Young's report caught immediate criticism from groups in Asia and the United States. Thuyen Nguyen, director of Vietnam Labour Watch, wrote:

Mr Young spent only 10 days visiting factories in China, Vietnam and Indonesia. His tours were conducted by management, and he talked to workers through Nike interpreters. Workers are not about to complain in front of the boss, especially in authoritarian countries where workers labelled troublemakers can be fired and jailed.[9]

Anita Chan, an Australian National University expert on Chinese shoe factories, said that in factories that produce for Nike and other brand name companies there is 'enforced overtime that exceeds the legal maximum, wages that are below the legal minimum, no days off for weeks on end, substantial fines for trivial offenses, [and] corporal punishment and physical abuse are common'.[10]

Groups independent of Nike soon issued reports with conclusions different to Young's. The Asia Monitor Resource Centre and the Hong Kong Christian Industrial Committee studied conditions in four major Chinese factories producing for Nike and Reebok. In a September 1997 report, they noted that 'practices and conditions at all factories in the survey systematically and grossly violated' the companies' own codes of conduct as well as Chinese labour law. Violations included excessive hours, forced overtime, denial of days off and wages below the legal minimum. 'Workers often are fired for being "too old" (more than 25). Even though Chinese law stipulates the right to a maternity leave, workers who become pregnant are fired,' the researchers said. Conditions also included exposure to toxic chemicals, high levels of dust and excessive heat, causing a variety of health problems.[11]

A leaked report from Nike's own auditor, Ernst & Young, revealed Vietnamese workers exposed to carcinogenic toluene at levels as high as 177 times the volume allowed by Vietnamese standards. According to *The New York Times*,

> The Ernst & Young report painted a dismal picture of thousands of young women, most under age 25, labouring 10½ hours a day, six days a week, in excessive heat and noise and in foul air, for slightly more than $10 a week. The report also found that workers with skin or breathing problems had not been transferred to departments free of chemicals and that more than half the workers who dealt with

dangerous chemicals did not wear protective masks or gloves.[12]

News of Nike's abusive practices spread on the Internet and among the growing network of anti-sweatshop activists at colleges, churches, unions and human rights groups. Even ESPN, the cable TV sports network, sent a crew to Vietnam in April 1998 to investigate production of the world's most popular athletic shoes. Though they gave a day's notice that they would visit a Nike contractor, the ESPN journalists were still able to tape two instances of supervisors doling out physical abuse to assembly line workers.[13] 'If Nike's contractors abuse workers in this way when they know they are being watched, we can only imagine what their behaviour is like in the absence of film crews,' observed the Campaign for Labour Rights, which coordinated the 18 April 1998 demonstrations.[14]

Over the course of the late 1990s, the Campaign used the Internet to disseminate research, action ideas, leaflets and analysis to a growing list of anti-sweatshop activists. Its call for an International Mobilization on Nike led to protests in fifty cities in the United States, fifteen cities in Canada, plus others in Finland, Australia, New Zealand and Chile. The Campaign recommended that protesters focus on Foot Locker, a retail chain that was Nike's biggest wholesale customer. The Labour Behind the Label Coalition, based in Toronto, added that Foot Locker was owned by Woolworth, whose Northern Group brands were at the time being produced in small shops that violated Canada's wage and hour laws. Many of the protesters also criticized the proposed Free Trade Area of the Americas (FTAA), which was being discussed that same weekend at a hemispheric summit in Santiago, Chile. The FTAA would lower trade barriers between 35 countries in the Western hemisphere, increasing the mobility of capital without giving any protection to worker or human rights.

Protests took place at shopping malls and downtown stores – both Foot Locker and Niketown. Participants included high school and college students, labour union activists and veterans of the Central America solidarity movement. Several featured street theatre, including people dressed up as rats, skunks and Santa Claus. In Portland, Oregon, a 12-foot high puppet representing Nike CEO Phil Knight danced and blew kisses with another giant puppet carrying the face of Bill Clinton on one side and Indonesian strongman Suharto on the other. Seven people wearing 'Ask Me Why Nike Sucks' T-shirts spent 90 minutes leafleting inside a Baltimore mall before getting kicked out and going to a second mall for another hour of leafleting.

According to a report from a Salt Lake City activist, protesters at the local Foot Locker outlet

> were mainly young people from the University of Utah and local high schools. Along with a sprinkling of trade union activists from the Oil, Chemical and Atomic Workers Union, the American Federation of State, County and Municipal Employees, and the United Steelworkers Union, the protesters created a lively picket line of signs, banners and chants criticizing Nike, sweatshops and NAFTA/'Free Trade'. JEDI Women, a local activist organization that advocates for low-income women, was an important sponsor of the protest. Brin Bon of JEDI Women expressed the spirit of building international solidarity among working people in her speech when she said 'We are not just doing this to boycott Nike but to help improve the lives of people everywhere.'[15]

The protests that rocked Seattle in the summer of 1999 and Washington, DC the following winter did not come out of nowhere. The anti-sweatshop actions were a crucial training ground and network-building opportunity for the coalition that emerged to counter free trade and financial deregulation worldwide.

The Footlocker Eight

In Manchester, New Hampshire, about thirty activists organized by the AFSC gathered at a Methodist Church and headed over to the mall to pass out leaflets near Foot Locker and the Disney Store. Eight of them planned to refuse to stop leafleting if they were so ordered. They had already attempted to meet with mall managers but the request had been turned down. They had participated in a non-violence training session, and had informed the police of their plans. They expected to be arrested.

The leaflet read:

> US workers are competing in a 'race to the bottom' with workers from poor countries like China, Vietnam, Haiti, Nicaragua and Mexico, where giant retail chains and clothing manufacturers go to find the lowest wages, weakest environmental protections and lowest taxes. In many cases, workers are subjected to starvation wages, 60-hour weeks and unsafe factories. When they stand up for their rights, they risk getting fired or worse. As sweatshops spread in poor countries, they are making a return in the United States and Canada as well.

The leaflet urged readers 'to send the companies a message', and stated that workers have a right to a living wage and decent working conditions, the right to unionize and bargain collectively, and the right to have their factories monitored by local human rights groups that could independently assess whether corporate codes of conduct were being observed. Facts about Nike production in Asia, Disney production in Haiti and J. C. Penney production in Nicaragua and China were featured. Along with addresses for the companies' chief executive officers (CEOs), the leaflet also urged readers to communicate with President Clinton about the Free Trade Area of the Americas.

Shoppers were generally interested in getting leaflets, and interest grew when Manchester police moved in. Several dozen leaflets had been distributed when the police ordered a halt, then arrested the eight activists who refused to stop leafleting. Charged with criminal trespass were a retired Unitarian Universalist minister, an executive board member of the State Employees Union, a veteran social studies teacher (who had taught the arresting officer in his class two decades earlier), a Haitian immigrant and daycare centre administrator, the student outreach coordinator of the American Federation of Labour–Congress of Industrial Organizations (AFL–CIO), the clerk of one of the state's Friends Meetings, a software engineer active in the Unitarian church, and me, the AFSC's New Hampshire Programme Coordinator and the action's primary organizer. Coming as they did from several parts of New Hampshire, their arrest captured even more local and statewide attention than the activists anticipated.

Coverage of the arrest was extensive, especially in daily and weekly papers. News stories on the arrests were followed by features on whether malls were free-speech zones or speech-free zones. The *Union Leader*, Manchester's notorious right-wing daily, editorialized in support of the civil disobedience action. 'We think the protesters have a good cause – trying to let people know about the exploitation of foreign workers who make clothing and footwear overseas that is sold at the mall,' wrote Editor-in-Chief Joseph McQuaid three days after the Mall arrests. 'Malls are today's equivalent of the town square of old.... Within reason, they ought to be places where peaceful protest can be carried out.' McQuaid followed with another supportive editorial three days later.

The *Monadnock Ledger*, a weekly from Peterborough, wrote: 'Shoppers have a right to know where and how the products they are purchasing are made, and at whose expense.' The student newspaper at Central High School editorialized in support of teacher Will Thomas. It was the *Concord Monitor* which first called the group the 'Footlocker Eight', expressing support both for the anti-sweatshop cause and the right to free speech inside the Mall.

The group's legal strategy was to use the courtroom as an anti-sweatshop symposium while arguing that the state constitution's free speech clause was applicable inside malls. The District Court judge was cooperative, at least as far as letting the defendants present their arguments. The case dragged on for thirteen months. After the initial procedural hearings, there were two hearings on the role of malls in economic and social life, followed by a hearing at which an expert witness argued the case against sweatshops and why mall leafleting was a lesser harm than the crimes being committed against workers. At the final hearing, the defendants were found guilty and gave short statements before sentencing. Public attention stayed with the case throughout. The judge found all eight guilty of criminal trespass and imposed a fine of $117 each, plus a short jail sentence suspended for good behaviour. Then the defendants filed an appeal with the state Supreme Court, and the Footlocker Eight stayed in the public eye for seven more months.

Radio talk shows invited Footlocker Eight members on as guests. High school teachers leading units on the constitution invited members into class to discuss free speech. Ripples from the case spread, even as the Footlocker activists were losing court decisions at the District, Superior and Supreme Court levels. Student activists at the University of New Hampshire disrupted a visit by Disney's corporate recruiters with information about the company's Haitian sweatshops; three were arrested. Folksinger Douglas Clegg, inspired by the Footlocker Eight action, wrote and recorded a song for his latest album. Reviewing a book about Belgian colonialism in Africa, the *Concord Monitor*'s editor wrote: 'Exploitation of the Third World remains common. The hunger for consumer goods in the West is so great that efforts to mitigate or expose this exploitation are routinely suppressed. This is the issue at the core of the current case of the Footlocker Eight in New Hampshire.'[16]

The New Hampshire Bar Association even based its annual 'mock trial' project on the Footlocker case. In 19 high schools and 15 middle schools, teams of students conducted courtroom role plays of a case based closely on that of the Footlocker Eight. To participate, students had to become familiar with sweatshops, free speech law and the practice of non-violent civil disobedience. Regional and statewide competitions, in which teams from different schools took the defence and prosecution positions, earned additional attention. The Sunapee Middle High School newspaper quoted the local team's faculty adviser saying the case 'pits the issues of Freedom of Speech and assembly against those of private property. It asks the students to think critically about these statutes.'[17]

The Anti-Sweatshop Movement

Across the United States, young people, who are intensely targeted by advertising for brands like Nike, have rebelled most effectively against the notion that brand loyalty is more important than citizenship. Identifying with the young women who work in the footwear and apparel sweatshops, college students in particular have energized the 'no sweat' movement and organized an effective national coalition, the United Students Against Sweatshops. Students across the United States have forced their colleges to adopt codes of conduct governing the production of clothes carrying the schools' logos. When many of the schools adopted codes initiated by the apparel companies themselves, Nike among them, students kept up the pressure and demanded codes that would go further. Issues in contention include whether factories can get away with paying the legal minimum wage when that provides less than a subsistence income, whether clothing companies will disclose the locations of factories that make their products, and how far the companies must go to demonstrate that they support the right of workers to organize unions.

Linked by the Internet, using tactics like street theatre, marches, leaflets and civil disobedience, the new anti-sweatshop movement has already made a difference in the suites as well as in the streets. Take Nike, for example. Three weeks after the 18 April 1998 mobilization, CEO Phil Knight went to the National Press Club in Washington, DC to announce reforms of the company's contractor policies. 'It has been said that Nike has single-handedly lowered the human rights standard for the sole purpose of maximizing profits,' he said. 'The Nike product has become synonymous with slave wages, forced overtime and arbitrary abuse. I truly believe that the American consumer does not want to buy products made in abusive conditions.' Knight pledged to raise the minimum age of new hires, to stop the use of toxic solvents, to raise air quality standards and for the first time to allow independent monitors into factories.[18]

That Knight made no pledge to raise wages or respect the rights of workers to unionize is an indication of where the movement has thus far fallen short of its goals. In general, consumer-based activism in wealthy countries has forced brand-name producers of apparel and footwear to demand that their contractors improve conditions. But wages in factories that produce goods for companies like Nike and retail chains like Wal-Mart still are too low to enable workers to escape poverty. And workers in Indonesia, Mexico, Nicaragua and Honduras are still struggling uphill to form independent unions and win collective bargaining agreements.

It is not enough to embarrass companies by revealing the gap between their public relations rhetoric and the real conditions in factories that produce their goods. The problems persist. A report issued by several labour and human rights groups in 2000 documented persistent sweatshop conditions at Asian factories making products for Nike. A survey of 3,500 Indonesian Nike workers documented physical and verbal abuse, forced overtime, poverty wages for shoe workers and starvation wages for apparel workers. An investigation of Chinese factories working under contract with Nike revealed 12 hour days and 7 day weeks at some plants, dangerous conditions, discriminatory hiring practices. And repression of workers' rights activists. 'The strategy that Nike appears to be pursuing is to take a number of high profile initiatives that portray the company in a positive light, while maintaining the core policies that allow it to profit off of horribly exploited labor,' the report concluded.[19]

In New Hampshire, activists are still leafleting, picketing and putting pressure on companies to clean up their acts. As part of the Campaign for Labor Rights' Rapid Action Network, they are

Living in Hope

increasingly focused on demonstrating solidarity with struggles in specific workplaces, not just demonstrating their own power as consumers. They are also looking at the economic arrangements established by international finance and trade organizations. And once again, the AFSC is waiting for the right time to return to the Mall of New Hampshire and assert the constitutional right to free speech and assembly.

Notes

1 National Labor Committee organizing materials.

2 Judith Lambert, deposition, 31 July 1998, p. 36.

3 J. B. Strasser and L. Becklund, *Swoosh: The Unauthorized Story of Nike and the Men Who Played There,* Harcourt Brace and Jovanovich, 1991.

4 *Ibid.*, p. 347.

5 Jardine, Fleming International Securities Limited, cited in a 1998 report of the Campaign for Labor Rights. Ironically, the Jardine Fleming report was distributed in Nike's own press packets by company PR reps doing damage control at colleges where Nike practices were under attack.

6 Campaign for Labor Rights alerts, 1 May, 18 June 1997

7 'Nike Tries to Quell Exploitation Charges,' *Wall Street Journal*, 25 June 1997.

8 Andrew Young, 'The Nike Code of Conduct,' GoodWorks International, 1997.

9 Thuyen Nguyen, letter to the editor, *New York Times*, 30 June 1997.

10 Dr Anita Chan, Australian National University (via internet).

11 'Working Conditions in Sports Shoe Factories in China Making Shoes for Nike and Reebok,' Asia Monitor Resource Centre and Hong Kong Christian Industrial Committee, 1997.

12 Steven Greenhouse, 'Nike Shoe Plant in Vietnam is Called Unsafe for Workers,' *New York Times*, 8 November 1997.

13 'Made in Vietnam, The American Sneaker Controversy: You Decide – Are they sweatshops?,' *ESPN*, 2 April 1998.

14 'ESPN Exposes Nike,' Campaign for Labor Rights *Newsletter*, June/July 1998.

15 Reports on the April 18 actions were distributed on the internet by the Campaign for Labor Rights.

16 'A dark past lives,' *Concord Monitor,* 9 October 1998.

17 Wendi Dowst, 'The Verdict is In: Mock Trial Was Worth While [sic]' *Sunapee Sentinel,* Sunapee Middle High School, 2000.

18 'Nike Pledges to End Child Labor and Apply U.S. Rules Abroad,' *The New York Times,* May 13, 1998.

19 'Sweatshops Behind the Swoosh,' Press for Change *et. al.*, 25 April 2000.

Giving Credit
Where Credit Is Due

Le Thi Lan was running a small business when she suddenly lost everything. Her husband was retired, and the family had no field land. 'We were so poor,' she says. 'My husband was very weak and couldn't continue teaching. Our four sons were small. We had nothing for the Tet (Lunar New Year) holiday. Friends and neighbours had to contribute money and rice to help us.'

At that point, Le Thi Lan borrowed from a private lender. 'Interest was very high at 5 per cent per month,' she remembers, 'but I still borrowed for my children's food and medicines. At that time, we stayed in a small, empty, thatched house.'

In 1996, Le Thi Lan turned to Quaker Service Vietnam's (QSV) credit programme, which provides small loans to the poor.

After borrowing my first loan, I made alcohol and used the paste to raise pigs. When the pigs were sold, I raised chickens. We have a small shop, where we sell everything. My husband goes to sell tobacco in the mountainous districts. With the profits from the small business and the pig raising, we were able to build a brick house in 1998 for 26 million dong (approximately US$1,857). Last year, we dug a well costing 650,000 dong (approximately $46). At present, all four sons go to school. Our first son will take his college entrance exams, and the smallest is in primary school.

Now, Le Thi Lan's family is considered among the rich in her village. She and her family have almost everything they need. The four sons are studying well, which makes Lan satisfied with her life.

Quaker Service Vietnam was the first non-government organization in Vietnam to run a credit programme. It set up the project in 1990 but dramatically revised the initial experiment in 1993 and began again in two of the poorer communes in Tinh Gia, one of the poorest districts in Thanh Hoa Province. The programme has since expanded to 46 communes in four districts. The design is similar to that of the Grameen Bank of Bangladesh in that it provides loans to poor people so they can raise livestock or start small businesses. However, the project's training component makes it different. Participants, who are all women, learn life skills that are transferable should market conditions change. Participants work together in the training programme, forming bonds of solidarity in the marketplace rather than competing against one another.

The revolving credit programme lends to the poorest of the poor, those who don't have the collateral to secure loans from banks. Its success can be measured in the stories of individuals such as Le Thi Lan and can be seen in the programme's remarkable repayment rate. In two of Vietnam's poorest districts, Tinh Gia and Ha Trung, the repayment rate has been over 98 per cent.

The goals of the programme are simple. By the end of the first year of borrowing the 'first-round loan', no one involved in the project should still be hungry. By the end of the second year, no one involved should still be poor. And by the end of the third year, borrowers or 'beneficiaries' should have become rich. 'Rich' is, of course, a relative term. 'Rich' in the credit project means the borrowers have enough food for their family all year, their children can go to school, and they can build and furnish brick houses.

Borrowing Money in Vietnam

Vietnam is in the midst of an economic transition that began in the late 1980s with *doi moi* (renovation) and the move to a market economy. Foreign investments are flowing into the country, and multilateral institutions are providing loans, which may well sentence Vietnam to the same debt spiral other developing countries experience. These changes have made money available, but usually only to the well-off. Generally speaking, everyone was poor before renovation. Now, Vietnam's market economy has created, as elsewhere in the world, an increasing gap between the rich and the poor. However, Vietnam's growth exhibits one significant difference: the poor are better off than before. Still, many have been left behind during this rapid economic change.

The State Bank of Vietnam never lends to individuals, and its conditions for borrowing are complicated. Private lenders have of course existed in Vietnam since time immemorial. During the 1930s and 1940s, private lenders' payment pressure was common and legal. They continued to operate after 1955, when lending became illegal. No one could force them to stop because they were the rich and many people needed their money. In some communities, these lenders were (and still are) criticized morally. However, no strong measures have been taken against them.

Poor people throughout the world have faced a similar dilemma: they can't borrow from the established banks, and private lenders' interest rates are prohibitive. The Grameen Bank, established in 1983 in Bangladesh, was one answer to this dilemma. Its revolving credit and loan programmes for the poor have become popular in developing countries. Although these programmes target the poor, they are run as banks. Money from the repaid loans returns to the bank. They are, in other words, businesses.

In 1995, the Vietnamese government established a similar programme, the Bank for the Poor, with assistance from Japanese development funds. The Bank for the Poor does not require collateral, but it does set up several obstacles that make it difficult for the very poor to borrow. To obtain a loan, borrowers must secure signatures from the head of their village and then from the commune People's Committee, which will never give a stamp to a very poor person. In fact, the very poor know better than to ask. The rate of interest in Bank-for-the-Poor loans is quite low. However, that figure is deceptive because borrowers must pay for their account papers, and then they must pay again and again for official stamps.

The Bank for the Poor is well funded. The loans are managed through the Farmers' Association, which has a board of managers. The managing board takes 3 per cent from the interest for the various associations involved (such as the Women's Union, the Gardeners' Association, etcetera). The more borrowers the board has, the more money goes into the various member association coffers. As a result, the Bank for the Poor will often lend to middle-income and rich people. In one district where QSV works, the district Bank lent 20 million dong (one-fifth of its capital, about $2,000 at that time) to the district chairman, leaving four-fifths of the funds for a population of 210,000 residents. Also, Bank-for-the-Poor loans go primarily to men.

Some of the Bank-for-the-Poor capital is never lent. The villages and communes create so much paper work for applicants for Bank loans that many borrowers are discouraged from applying. In one district, excessive paperwork resulted in 500 million VND (US$44,000) not being disbursed. In Ha Tinh Province, the figure is ten times higher. The problem lies in the locality's inability to absorb the funds.

A Different Approach

The QSV programme differs from Grameen Bank-style programmes in several key ways. The money returns to the community, not to the grantor. Training is a key component. Even the participants are different. QSV beneficiaries are all poor women whose families lack food for at least three months of the year. They may be people with disabilities, but they must be able to work at a self-chosen project, and they must be willing to work hard. They and their family members should not suffer from addictions, including gambling. And they must volunteer for the project. QSV works in what standard banks would consider to be high-risk areas. These risks are not simply financial. Women in Vietnam's poor areas face not only starvation but also the threat of being induced into trafficking rings with China, where a gender imbalance has created a dearth of marriageable wives.

Once accepted, the participants must join a training course in order to understand the programme's principles and requirements. Project members attend monthly meetings. They learn how to save money and how to make instalment repayments. They also choose new borrowers and share work experiences. Project Management Boards (PMBs) at the three levels (district, commune and village centre) record the new payments, do the bookkeeping and report monthly. During the past six years, QSV has organized many training courses for PMB members to improve their capacity to manage loan projects. In addition, QSV organizes visits for PMB members from each district to model credit projects run by other international NGOs and the National Women's Union. QSV directly supervises the implementation of the project in the communes, visits beneficiaries, supplies the loans, issues documents and helps the Project Management Board in training participants.

Credit and savings are very effective development programmes. On the face of it, they also seem to be the easiest of programmes: you simply give poor people money. In fact, credit and savings are the *hardest* programmes to execute successfully. Most development organizations new to credit and savings ignore the essential training component. As a result, most programmes ultimately fail. The participants never become anything other than borrowers, and the overall programme does not become sustainable. QSV's greatest contribution at the macro level is constantly to raise this point with foreign donors who think credit and savings is an easy antidote to poverty.

Another difference is the relationship between Quaker Service and the Women's Union in Vietnam. The savings/credit project is implemented by the Women's Union at three levels: village, commune and district. The district Women's Union branches keep close contact with QSV in monitoring the project. In recent years, with QSV support, district Women's Union staff members have also done the training for borrowers. QSV provides training for the bookkeepers. This cooperative relationship strengthens the Women's Union, and the number of women who join the union has increased. The roles and prestige of the Women's Union at different levels has improved. Through the project activities, the district and commune Women's Union chapters have improved their capacity in economic management and in implementing savings/ credit projects.

The Mechanics of the Programme

By the end of June 1999, the QSV savings and credit programme had 8,052 borrowers with a total of outstanding loans amounting to approximately $250,000. By March 2001, there were 11,264 borrowers. The breakdown of the project loan structure is as follows:

- Savings fund;
- Loan repayment;
- Loan interest.

From October 2000, the interest rate charged on a loan has been 1.5 per cent per month. The repayment is made on a monthly basis. The loan duration is twelve months. In risk cases, such as when an animal dies, the borrowers may extend their repayment for three months. However, if they fail to vaccinate their animals, their loans are neither extended nor forgiven. The loans increase in size with each step. The first loan is 500,000 dong (approximately $34.25), the second loan is 700,000 dong (approximately $47.95) and the third loan is 1,000,000 dong (approximately $68.50).

The interest income is divided into several categories. Half of the interest received goes to increasing the size of the loan fund. One quarter goes to pay local administrators of the fund, including the commune and village project manager, accountant, and cashier. Ten per cent goes for stationery. Five per cent goes to the district Women's Union for training borrowers and monitoring. Five per cent goes to the commune Women's Union Fund, and five per cent to the village Women's Union Fund. These funds are used for death-day commemorations, funerals, weddings and small gifts for excellent participants.

All borrowers are required to practise savings for three months before receiving loans. First, they are trained in the concept of savings and come to understand why they are required to save regularly. Before the scheme is implemented, participants must save in groups of five persons. By the end of June 1999, the total amount of savings in QSV projects was 470,954,000 dong (approximately $33,640), or about 13 per cent of the original loan.

The interest rate paid for savings money is 1 per cent per month or 12 per cent per year. Every borrower must make a monthly contribution to her savings. The group members decide the amount of savings. Normally, this amount depends on their crops. The group heads are responsible for collecting the savings money. After the collection, this money is transferred to the PMB at the commune level. However, all savings money is re-loaned to new borrowers on the very day of monthly collection. All members of the project can borrow money from the savings fund. The duration of this loan is one year, and the interest is 1.5 per cent per month. All borrowing procedures are the same as for the original loans. After two years in the project, borrowers may withdraw their savings. Borrowers who leave the project can withdraw their savings at that time.

Living in Hope

The accounting for this programme is challenging. In Bank-for-the-Poor loans the principal is repaid after three years. This makes the bank's bookkeeping easy. However, QSV beneficiaries pay their loans back in monthly instalments. Although this reduces borrowers' fear of a huge payment at some future date, managers and participants must pay closer attention to accounting details.

Learning about the mechanics of savings and credit is part of the training. The savings funds encourage women to change their behavioural patterns, and the payback requirements create sustain-ability. The Group Fund also provides a community support mechanism in case of emergencies. In addition to training and practice on specific project management techniques (how to select borrowers, how to set up borrowing groups, how to choose a management board, how to launch savings, and bookkeeping), the training also focuses on basic organizational skills, including communication, cooperation, decision making and leadership models. As a result, women have begun to take a more active role in household and village decision making.

Success Stories

'Before having the project loan, we used to lack food,' Nguyen Thi Minh says. She lives in Thong Nhat village in Tinh Gia district. Her daughter is eighteen years old; her son, who is sixteen, has a nerve disease.

> We lived on two sao (1,000 square metres) of paddy field, without an extra job. I borrowed my first loan in 1996 to raise a pig. After selling the pigs for 1,400,000 dong, I used 100,000 dong for my daughter to set up a small business, 500,000 dong to sell peanuts and the rest to buy steel and rock for the foundation of my new brick house.
>
> Our village often 'hosts' typhoons. The storms blow our thatch

houses away. We all dream of having a brick house. After borrowing a second loan of 500,000 dong, I continued to raise pigs. With the profits from pig raising and our small business, we built a brick house in 1997 for 16 million dong ($1,143). Although we are not a well-off family, we have a better life and a solid house.

Before joining the credit loan project, Mrs Minh had to borrow money for food at the very high interest rate of 5 per cent per month. Because of the project loan, she is now able to generate income.

Most of the loan money for the programme has been used for appropriate purposes and has brought positive economic results, with increased income for the women and their families. Most loans were invested in agricultural production and fishing. Funds were used to raise pigs, chickens, ducks and fish, to purchase fertilizer and pesticides, and to buy materials for providing services and setting up small trading businesses. The project provided extra loans for reinvestment in emergency cases, where individuals lost their investments through no fault of their own.

Most of the project activities generated a profit. Eighty per cent of project households increased their income. Before joining the project, many poor women in Hai Ninh, a coastal commune of Tinh Gia district, were jobless; now, they have a good income from investing their project loan in fishing. Each group consists of 34–45 members. Fishing people can work only five months a year, not counting days lost to storms, strong wind, cold, rain and heavy waves. Spread over the entire year, the women's average daily profit was 7,000 dong ($0.48). In contrast, farmers who worked twelve months made an average daily profit of 1,500 dong ($0.10).

With loans, many households reduced the number of months when they lacked food. Many households improved the quality of their meals. Some households built new houses, drying yards, wells and pigpens. Many households repaired their houses bought new productive equipment, or purchased equipment for the family such as bicycles, beds, cupboards, tables, chairs, radios and television sets. When the family economy improved, the parents paid more attention to their children's heath and education. Many children in project households not only have books and other resources for their studies but also new clothes. Several families have sent their grown-up children to vocational training.

Through group meetings, the women improved their knowledge of raising animals and managing their family economy. Many project participants have undertaken new work opportunities, which have brought them greater income. The savings step trained the women in this habit, allowed them to generate their own additional loan funds, and helped participants make more effective family expenditure plans. It also helped the women create a local Group Fund.

The programme helped women improve their roles in their families as well as in their villages. The women have their own names in the borrowers' list. Husbands and children help the women work in the house as well as in the field. Some husbands attended the group meetings when their wives were sick.

Community Impact

The project has contributed to hunger eradication and poverty alleviation and to creating jobs for poor women. It has also reduced the premature selling of rice harvests in order to pay private lenders. Formerly, many farmers sold their rice or corn prematurely at below-harvest rates to buy food. But nowadays, few farmers do this, except when facing emergencies such as education payments, or escrow-guarantee ls or children working abroad.

and friendship have improved. Project par-
r relationships and willingly help each other

out of difficulties. Project members participate in social activities and charity work. For example, at the beginning of the 1997–8 school year, the members in Vinh Tan commune, Vinh Loc district, gave 120,000 dong for books to poor students in Da But village. Since 1996, QSV staff members have made many visits to the project area to talk with the beneficiaries and with the local people. They have learned that project loans were highly appreciated.

As with any programme, there have been challenges. Some borrowers do not always attend the monthly meetings. Many participants believe that making their monthly repayments is enough and that they don't need to go to a meeting. In some project communes, the savings plans generate small amounts, with some participants contributing only 500 or 1,000 dong monthly.

The QSV projects do manage to avoid one of the chief challenges facing revolving credit programmes: new divisions of wealth and poverty in the countryside. Farmers tend to compare and complain when one area has a project and another does not. But QSV's target beneficiaries are the poorest of the poor. QSV does a survey first and then chooses the project site according to QSV criteria:

- Two-thirds of the population in each village/commune must be poor;

- The people must lack food from three months upwards.

QSV doesn't consider those who lack food for two months as poor. With clear criteria, the number of complaints falls dramatically.

As a result of Quaker Service credit programmes, local private lenders in QSV project sites can no longer charge exorbitant interest rates as before. Now, the poor have access to capital. These activities helped build the Women's Union, whose membership roles have increased dramatically because these loans are obtainable only through the Union. Activities at the monthly repayment meetings provide good opportunities for other technical transfer information about raising livestock and growing new seed and fruit-tree varieties.

The old days of the command economy had a certain kind of security. Economic life was predictable: everyone was poor. Now, Vietnam's market economy is beholden to both local and global forces. Predictability has vanished. A new joint-venture plant may bring jobs but its effluent may ruin farmland and fishing beds. A coffee blight in Colombia can raise international prices and fill the coffers of Vietnamese growers, but equally, a rice farmer's bumper harvest in Vietnam may actually bring decreased income if Thai and US farmers also reap good yields.

Vietnamese are known for being practical and innovative. The QSV small-scale credit and savings programme builds on those qualities by providing skills and the means for poor women to increase their capital. Poor women can become more entrepreneurial. Through training, they build skills, capital and a community that can move on to other opportunities when market forces change.

Responding to Debt in Africa

Njoki Njoroge Njehu

In July 2001 activists and campaigners from nine Eastern Africa countries gathered in Nairobi, Kenya at a weeklong seminar designed to create a regional network, coordinate public education initiatives, mobilize grassroots organizers and other stakeholders, and learn from strong regional networks and campaigns, especially in southern Africa. The East African Regional Seminar on Debt, like many initiatives by African civil society, was an affirmation of both the critical work that individuals and groups are doing and the importance of working in broad and strong coalitions. Much of the seminar time was spent on mutual education and strategy sessions.

The East African Regional Seminar on Debt was another step in a series of initiatives by people in the Global South who continue to struggle for justice. The South–South Summit on Debt[1] had been the first such gathering initiated and led by activists and campaigners from the Global South. In November 1999 over 150 participants from 40 countries gathered outside Johannesburg for the South–South Summit on Debt, convened by Jubilee South and hosted by Jubilee 2000 South Africa. The Summit was designed to bring together campaigners for debt cancellation from countries of the Global South – in Africa, Asia–Pacific and Latin America–Caribbean – to forge a common approach and strategies as part of the global Jubilee movement. Declaring that we DON'T OWE – WON'T PAY!, the participants reaffirmed a long-standing view that the Global South is a creditor not a debtor given the historical context of imperialism, slavery, colonialism and neo-colonialism. The peoples of the Global South are owed a great debt by the perpetrators and beneficiaries of the resulting exploitation and oppression.

Jubilee South brought together campaigns for debt cancellation in nearly fifty countries. Its formation represented an unprecedented level of cooperation and exchange on issues of economic justice among the different regions of the Global South. The excitement generated at the Johannesburg meeting by the breadth of representation, as well as by the level of agreement that was achieved, was tremendous. If Jubilee South's greatest achievement undoubtedly lies in its creation of a vibrant network of groups that continue to exchange information and strategies, no one should underestimate, either, the hard work it got through in formulating common positions to increase the power of Southern civil society in global debates.

The international Jubilee movement – encompassing Jubilee South and the national campaigns that comprise it, the Jubilee 2000 campaigns of the Northern countries, and the successor organizations founded after the end of 2000 (a date which did not change the name or composition of Jubilee South) – has had remarkable success in turning one of the driest topics imaginable, international debt, into a popular cause in dozens of countries, a steady concern in the financial media and a set of demands that the international financial institutions and the wealthy industrialized country governments simply could not ignore. The Jubilee movement is an often-overlooked but indispensable contributing factor to the seemingly sudden blossoming of the international movement for global justice, usually associated with the Seattle protests at the World Trade Organization meeting in late 1999 (indeed, the Jubilee events in Seattle, including a candlelight march in the rain, brought perhaps 10,000 people together on the eve of the main day of actions, and set the stage for the events to come).

The Jubilee movement has achieved real shifts in public policy at the international financial institutions and in wealthy-country governments. All the member governments of the Group of Seven (G7) industrialized nations (the US, the UK, Canada, Italy, Japan, Germany and France) committed by 2000 to provide, under one set of circumstances or another, 100 per cent cancellation of bilateral debts. They also agreed in 1999 to changes in the IMF/World Bank debt-management scheme (the Heavily Indebted Poor Countries Intiative, or HIPC) – changes which signalled a rebuke to the institutions for their slow pace and miserly behaviour with regard to debt.

The changes and the policy shifts have not gone nearly far enough, however. Huge debt tallies continue to prevent governments from choosing their own priorities and funding the programmes that would best develop their countries. Even countries that have received 'generous' debt relief find that they are still paying enormous amounts on debt service. Jubilee South's position is that the very logic of debt – the idea that the accumulated damages of imperialism over the years have no bearing on how today's debts are calculated; the notion that it is appropriate for the most impoverished people in the world to pay back loans which went to corrupt dictators and inefficient projects – needs to be questioned. The need for a strong Jubilee movement is just as urgent as ever.

Debt in Africa

Campaigners for social and economic justice acknowledge that one of the greatest challenges facing the African continent is the unbearable and unjust burden of debt claimed by international lending agencies and creditors such as the IMF, the World Bank and the Group of Seven member countries to multinational banks and other creditors. To repay these debts African governments continue to divert scarce financial resources away from basic services such as education, health care, food security, sustainable livelihoods, safe water, environmental protection, and strengthening the social safety net.

Debt is what subjects African countries to the mandates of the IMF and World Bank. Debt is what diverts resources from health and education spending. And debt is what inhibits productive investment. Any plan to benefit Africa must include comprehensive debt cancellation for sub-Saharan Africa.

- In 1999 sub-Saharan Africa (excluding South Africa, with its anomalous history and unusual level of industrialization) owed US$203 billion, which is three times the annual value of its exports.[2]

- In 1996 Africa paid $2.5 billion more in debt servicing than it got in new long-term loans and credits.[3] The transfer of wealth is flowing from impoverished countries in the Global South to enriched countries and creditors in the North. The notion that the North is pouring money into basket-case, corrupt countries is mostly a myth.

- Sub-Saharan Africa's GNP *per capita* is $308 but the *per capita* external debt is higher, at $365.[4] Debt servicing accounts for about 20 per cent of Africa's export income.[5] And sub-Saharan African governments spend four times more on interest payments than on health care.[6] In the late 1990s Zambia was spending $37 million on primary education while at the same time devoting $1.3 billion to debt payments.[7]

- From 1990 to 1995, the 33 African countries officially classified as heavily-indebted and poor experienced forest loss 50 per cent greater than that in better-off countries, and 140 per cent greater than the world average during the same period.[8] And as Kenyan environmentalist Professor Wangarî Maathai has observed, the Sahara has been spreading north because it is being created in every backyard.

- The persisting huge debts are a major disincentive to productive investment in the region.

- Of 36 million people living with HIV/AIDs worldwide, 25 million live in Africa.[9] Over 22 million people have died of HIV/AIDS worldwide, 17 million of them in sub-Saharan Africa.[10] About 13 million children have been orphaned by AIDS worldwide; 12 million of these orphans are in sub-Saharan Africa. It is further estimated that by the year 2010 there will be 40 million AIDs orphans in Africa.[11]

It is the poor people of the indebted countries, those who have benefited the least from the loans, who end up paying the debt through the diversion of scarce resources to debt servicing, and through the restraining effects of the IMF/World Bank austerity programmes. These structural adjustment programmes, which have been imposed repeatedly on almost every country in Africa since the early 1980s, mandate massive lay-offs, sharp reductions in credit, increased taxes and higher interest rates, privatization of government-owned companies, cuts in spending on health and education and currency devaluation. Average real wages decreased in 26 out of 28 African countries surveyed during the 1980s. Cuts in health spending have led inevitably to an increase in infant mortality; as a result, African children were expected to account for about 40 per cent of infant deaths worldwide by the year 2000. Millions of small farmers, especially women, have been devastated by IMF-induced cuts in credit and agricultural services. Some 40 per cent of the population suffer from some degree of malnutrition.

According to the United Nations Development Programme (UNDP), cuts in health spending mean that 19,000 children around the world, nearly half of them African, continue to die every day from curable and preventable diseases and thousands of mothers die in childbirth. Cuts in food subsidies and turning fertile lands over to production of flowers or cotton or coffee for export mean millions more children suffering from malnutrition and dying from starvation. The promotion of an export-oriented model of production condemns millions of children to work in fields – cutting cane, or picking coffee, tea and cotton – instead of going to school.

International debt is a devastating burden for African peoples to bear, and our future and heritage has been mortgaged for generations to come. The productive capacity of communities, countries and the entire region is being disabled across the board. For instance, in the midst of the HIV/AIDS pandemic the capacity for providing health care has been decimated – in 1981, there were 10,000 people for every doctor in Kenya; by 1994 that ratio had gone up to nearly 22,000 people per doctor. In Uganda, there were 661 people for every hospital bed in 1981, while in 1994 there were 1,092 for every bed. In Ghana, a country often touted as an example of how structural adjustment can work, the percentage of infants with low birth weight went from 5 per cent in 1988 to 17 per cent in the period 1992–5. Many children die young (17 per cent before the age of five in Africa) and their educational opportunities are reduced each year. By the IMF's own admission, in African countries with structural adjustment programmes, *per capita* education spending actually declined by 0.7 per cent annually between 1986 and 1996.[12]

However, within the context of these devastating social and economic crises, African peoples have been fighting. African peoples, like peoples throughout the Global South, 'still rise'! They have and are surviving, despite conditions of extreme hardship and devastation. We peoples of the Global South have chosen to face our problems, to seek solutions, to propose alternatives, and to say clearly – as the World Social Forum (held in Porto Alegre, Brazil in January 2001 and again in January 2002) proclaims – that 'Another World Is Possible.' Another world is absolutely necessary.

Looking Ahead

Jubilee South has provided leadership and a framework for campaigners and campaigns in African, Asia–Pacific and Latin America–Caribbean countries to articulate their demands and to shape the very nature of the campaign worldwide. The role of Jubilee South has not been an easy one, nor have the initiatives of those most directly affected always been welcomed by some campaigners in the international Jubilee movement. The Jubilee South positions that participants articulated at the South–South Summit on Debt, and which continue to be sharpened, revolve around the following points:

- Rejection – of the HIPC Initiative and of the HIPC classification which is based on an arbitrary IMF and World Bank rationale. The HIPC Initiative is an IMF/World Bank incentive for structural adjustment with the promise of 'debt relief'. At the 1999 G7 meeting in Cologne, Germany Jubilee South declared the HIPC initiative to be a poisoned chalice.

- Repudiation – a demand that governments in the Global South disclaim the debts as odious and illegitimate in view of the tremendous ecological and historical debt owed *to* the Global South by the North for centuries of exploitation, slavery and colonialism.

- Restitution – a demand that the agencies and individuals in lending agencies complicit in abetting corruption, as well as their accomplices in borrowing countries and in private banks, be prosecuted, with full cooperation from the institutions, and that those responsible, including the institutions, recover and return stolen wealth and provide compensation for unrecoverable stolen resources.

- Reparations a demand for the North to pay the South for the damage done by the machinery of exploitation and debt.

The challenge for campaigners in the North concerns what they must do to support these Southern demands. While Africans struggle and seek out their future and the future of their continent, it would serve us well to have the support of the rest of the human family. We need opportunities for people and countries to determine their own future, not more hoops to jump through like the new Poverty Reduction Strategy Process (PRSP) of the IMF and World Bank. We need grants to allow African peoples to follow dreams of development without mortgaging their grandchildren's future to more loans and therefore more debt. We need credit for farmers growing food crops, not more land reform programmes designed by bureaucrats who have never visited a small rural farm, let alone been a farmer. We need access to basic health care, not more user fees which result in many children dying because their parents cannot afford three cents for immunization. Instead of more reforms Africans need clinics stocked with drugs and staffed by well-trained workers; schools with textbooks and trained teachers; safe water for all instead of privatization contracts for multinational corporations; free public education for African children, just as for children in the US; policies that put people before profits. There is a proven track record of investment and political will in the international campaigns against polio and smallpox, and the campaign to immunize the world's children against the major vaccine-preventable diseases (measles, tetanus, diphtheria, whooping cough, polio, etcetera). We went from covering about 5 per cent of the world's children in 1980 to 80 per cent in 1990, and have saved about three million children a year. We know what needs to be done; we know how to do it and, in a number of instances, we have done it. The same can be true for Africa. African peoples need solidarity, not charity. Solidarity can mean a chance to succeed and to live with dignity.

Notes

1 Visit the Jubilee South web site for details on the South–South Summit: <www.jubileesouth.net>

2 World Bank, *Global Development Finance*, 1998.

3 *Ibid.*

4 *Ibid.*

5 *Ibid.*

6 Web site of the European Network on Debt and Development: <www.one world.org/eurodad/g7_gb.htm>

7 *Ibid.*

8 UN Food and Agriculture Organization, *State of the World's Forests*, 1997,

9 Web site of The Hunger Project: <www.thp.org>

10 *Ibid.*

11 *Ibid.*

12 *The IMF and the Poor*, Pamphlet Series No. 52 (Washington: IMF, 1998), p. 9.

Dignity Is the Reward

Ricardo Hernández

> Yes, turn your back on the sweet sunlight. Tear open the gates that others shrink from approaching. The time has come to show by your deeds that man in moral courage is equal to the gods, bold enough to face that dark horrific cavern and force his way to the narrow passage, girt with flames of hell, and do it serenely, even at the risk of lapsing into nothingness.
>
> *Faust* (Goethe)[1]

Today, Carrizo Manufacturing no longer exists, although it once employed 900 workers. Juany Cázares and Paty Leyva were two of them. They used to sew Disney children's pyjamas and men's pants for Carrizo, working at breakneck speed. By February 1999, however, they noticed that production was decreasing. Entire shifts were sent home for days, which then stretched into weeks.

Juany and Paty live in Piedras Negras in the Mexican state of Coahuila. They have three children each, and their husbands have also worked for many years in maquiladoras like Carrizo. maquiladoras are plants located on the Mexican side of the border with the United States under foreign (primarily US) ownership. They assemble finished goods for export, also mainly to the United States. The maquiladora industry is a cornerstone of the Mexican economy, particularly since the implementation of the North American Free Trade Agreement (NAFTA), and the Mexican government is the industry's very enthusiastic supporter. Today there are more than 3,000 maquiladoras, 80 per cent of them located in Mexico's northern border states. Together, these firms employ almost one and a half million people. Maquiladora production represents approximately 45 per cent of the country's total exports. In 2000, 89 per cent of that total went to the United States, amounting to US$148 billion.

Carrizo was a wholly owned subsidiary of the New York–based Salant Corporation. Facing an extremely competitive environment as a result of the global dismantling of trade barriers, apparel and textile producers are constantly restructuring their operations – buying and selling businesses, licensing new brand names and discontinuing others, outsourcing most of their manufacturing, moving from one country to another, repositioning themselves in global markets, and focusing their product lines. At the time this story began, Carrizo made John Henry and Manhattan dress shirts, Disney and Warner Brothers blanket sleepers, and Oshkosh B'Gosh pyjamas, as well as slacks for Sears and Roebuck's Canyon River Blues label.

Workers versus the Company, the Labour Authorities — and the Union

As the weeks went by in February 1999, Carrizo workers saw their hours cut back so much that they were taking home only half of their normal pay. Rumours circulated that the company was going to declare bankruptcy. Juany Cázares, Paty Leyva and others at Carrizo began to mobilize, warning their fellow workers of what was undoubtedly coming: the closing of the plant and the consequent loss of 900 jobs. They challenged the leader of their union local, a woman who was urging workers to understand the company's financial problems. Mexico's principal labour confederation, whose affiliates include thousands of union locals all over the country, has historically been aligned with Mexico's government and its economic policies, which have strongly supported a favourable climate for foreign investment.

Meanwhile, Carrizo managers had already come to an understanding with the local labour authorities and union leadership.

They hoped to avoid fulfilling the company's legally mandated obligation to make substantial severance payments to laid-off workers. The powerful tripartite alliance of company, union and government was resolved to pay as little as possible. Workers were told that if they complained they could lose everything, because the company would simply leave the country without paying anything at all.

Under Mexican labour law, severance payments are determined by adding various entitlements to the base salary then multiplying the sum by the length of service. At Carrizo, the company relied on manipulated calculations that eliminated many workers' benefits. For the Carrizo workers to derive their own figures was not easy. The workers were nonetheless able to figure out the amounts owed to them because previously, over the course of months or even years, they had participated in study groups organized by the Border Committee of Women Workers (Comité Fronterizo de Obreras or CFO), a grassroots organization of maquiladora workers. The CFO is a partner of the Mexico–US Border Programme of the American Friends Service Committee (AFSC). AFSC helped initiate the CFO twenty years ago, becoming a pioneer in seeking concrete solutions to the problems associated with the integration of the two countries' economies, a process which has had a considerable negative impact on the lives of women workers and their communities.

Over the years, the AFSC and the CFO have learned a lot from their direct contact with the human face of globalization. Thousand of workers supported by both organizations have achieved many benefits: correct payment for extra hours; just severance payments; profit sharing; elimination of safety risks in the workplace; installation of extractors to remove hazardous fumes and dust; halting of inappropriate behaviour by supervisors; and wage raises in small and big companies.

On a world scale, the Mexico–US border has served as a laboratory for free trade over the 36 years that have passed since the first maquiladoras opened. As far back as 1965, employers and government officials from both countries decided to facilitate the establishment of 'twin plants' on both sides of the border, a job creation strategy designed ultimately to discourage Mexican migration to the United States. In fact, maquiladoras have never served as a disincentive to migration; the jobs have never been good ones. Nor has the 'twin plant' concept ever become a reality.

Juany and Paty had worked for 13 and five years, respectively, for Carrizo Manufacturing. They liked working there, partly because that maquiladora paid better wages in comparison to others in town. These better conditions existed not because Salant executives in New York were unusually compassionate people, but because the rank and file had struggled persistently to improve working conditions and ensure the implementation of their collective bargaining agreement, with or without the support of union officials.

Juany and Paty were part of that collective and largely invisible effort. For more than a month, they and many other members of the CFO set out to meet with hundreds of their co-workers, one by one, to make them aware of the deceit that was being practised against them.

Corporate Chicanery

Since my office is based in the United States, the CFO asked me to obtain more information about the finances of Salant Corporation. Salant does not have a web site; even if it did, it would not include the information needed by the workers. It was by checking documents filed with the US Securities and Exchange Commission (SEC) that I learned that Salant had decided to focus on its Perry Ellis line of men's apparel and to sell its Children's Apparel Group as well as other licences and distribution centres in the United States, including one in Eagle Pass, a small Texas town that lies just across the border from Piedras Negras. Both cities are two and a half hours south of San Antonio, Texas.

I searched through hundreds of pages to find the information that would best serve the workers and translated it into Spanish, adding written summaries that the CFO was then able to use in its meetings and vigils outside the plant. In several telephone consultations, we discussed the implications of this information and possible scenarios for the Salant Corporation's restructuring plan. Part of the CFO's campaign to expose the company's actions involved making daily telephone calls to a popular radio talk show in Piedras Negras. One day I myself called the talk show from 2,000 miles away in Philadelphia, Pennsylvania, to provide information about Salant. Together, the workers and the AFSC were able to counter the misinformation spread by management and union officials.

In March 1999 Carrizo Manufacturing closed its doors. The true motive for the closure was neither bankruptcy nor relocation to a place with cheaper labour. Under its restructuring plan, Salant was simply selling all operations unrelated to Perry Ellis. Its financial problems would be solved by an US$85 million line of credit approved by a commercial services group. Official documents filed by Salant with the SEC clearly stated that Salant's restructuring would not affect its ability to meet its obligations to clients, suppliers or employees.

A few days later, the workers' suspicions were confirmed. At the entrance to the plant was posted a list of their names along with the amount of their severance payments as determined by Carrizo management. The amounts posted fell as much as 75 per cent below what the workers were legally entitled to. Things came to a head as the workers were informed they had only a few days to pick up their severance cheques. Some 400 workers sought to convince the other 500 not to pick up their cheques, in order to preserve their right to demand the full severance payment required by Mexican law. Some of the workers did not understand their legal rights; others desperately needed the money after two months of taking home only half of their normal pay.

It was a moment of great tension. All of the workers agreed on the importance of resisting, but they were also afraid that the company would leave the country without paying them anything. In the end, all 900 agreed to accept the payments, while resolving to continue their movement through other means. When the workers picked up their cheques at the offices of the local labour board, they were asked to sign a sheet of paper listing their names and the amount of each cheque. This list, labour officials explained, was supposed to keep track of disbursements.

Their Own Best Advocates

In the succeeding weeks and months, the extent of Carrizo's duplicity was revealed. For example, Antonia Figueroa, who had worked for Carrizo for 27 years, received a severance payment of US$3,900. According to the CFO's calculations, she was legally entitled to $15,806. Many other workers were in the same situation. The company's arithmetic was especially prejudicial to workers with the most seniority. Furthermore, at the local labour board, Juany and Paty found out that a cover letter had been added to the lists signed by all the workers. This letter stated that by signing they were resigning from Carrizo and waiving their right to pursue any further legal action against the company.

The workers decided to sue the Salant Corporation in the Mexican courts. They assembled documentation for 185 workers and consulted with several Mexican experts in labour law. As strategy for the case was developed, CFO representatives, especially Julia Quiñonez, the group's coordinator and a former maquiladora worker herself, ended up explaining to the lawyers how to interpret Mexico's labour code as well as the scope of the law. Among other things, this case demonstrated that the CFO's knowledge of labour rights in the maquiladoras is the most sophisticated in all of Mexico. Most important, the people who hold that knowledge and who communicate it best are maquiladora workers themselves: they are their own best advocates.

By mid-1999, the Carrizo workers had decided they had to go to New York City to meet with Salant's top management. AFSC's task was to arrange the meeting. The company totally refused to meet with us, but Juany, Paty and Julia set off nonetheless on a speaking tour of Washington, Philadelphia and New York.

Some labour rights advocates in Mexico asked the CFO representatives why they wanted to meet with Salant executives, since they had already signed off on their own resignations. Carrizo workers had earned $90 a week, considerably more than the average of $35 earned by most maquiladora workers along the border — so why were they complaining? The women of the CFO responded that they wanted not only to obtain a just severance payment, but above all to let the executives know that the workers were fully aware of how the company had tried to cheat them. They also wanted to set a precedent in the overall struggle for workers' dignity.

'Family' Meeting in New York City

As we tried to obtain a meeting with Salant executives, AFSC and the CFO gathered expressions of support from the Interfaith Centre for Corporate Responsibility, members of the US Congress, the AFL–CIO, and the garment workers' union, UNITE! When we arrived in New York City on 18 October 1999, however, Salant was still saying no.

The following day, with just a few hours notice, Salant finally agreed to a meeting. UNITE! officials had established contact with company executives the night before, and the firm had also received a fax from several members of the US Congress expressing concern for the Mexican women. Salant was facing pressure on several fronts.

Perhaps to avoid any legal repercussions, the executives asked to meet us not at Salant's offices, but at UNITE! headquarters in Manhattan. We were expecting to meet only with Louis Matielli, the company's vice-president, who had already stipulated that he would listen to the workers but would not negotiate anything. Salant's chief executive officer, Michael Setola, however, unexpectedly showed up.

At the meeting itself, Juany Cázares and Paty Leyva were a little nervous at first because of the confrontational demeanour of Setola and Matielli, who looked as if they had been expecting to meet the lawyers of a rival corporation. As the meeting unfolded, however, not only did Juany, Paty and Julia not become intimidated, they also found the words to tell their story in a convincing and powerful way. Reflecting on her thirteen years in Carrizo, Juany commented:

> the former American manager at Carrizo used to tell us 'I want you all to feel comfortable here because we are all family' and I believed him, and for that reason I used to reach 200 per cent of my production quota for the company. That's why I don't think the severance payments we received were just.

Julia spoke about the many loyal employees who had dedicated a good part of their lives to the company and who were the ones most affected by the insufficient payments. As he listened to the women, Setola seemed to soften up. He said that he would investigate the case of the 185 workers and acknowledged receipt of the CFO's petition for extra compensation.

In the end, however, Michael Setola – a corporate manager who in 2000 earned a base salary of $700,000 and received a $650,000 bonus (together these sums are 271 times greater than the year's pay of Juany Cázares); and who was also provided with an automobile allowance of $680 a month, a housing allowance of $3,000 per month and stock options – did not compensate

Antonia Figueroa and other Mexican workers with many years of seniority. The total requested by the workers was $800,000, which represents only 1.43 percent of Salant's annual gross profit of 56 million in 1999.

From Disney to Dockers

The CFO's legal complaint was ultimately filed with the Mexican labour board. Since labour boards have proved partial to business interests, it was not a surprise that after one year it was decided that there were no grounds for a favourable outcome in the workers' case against Carrizo. Still, what Juany and Paty learned about their power and own capacity was a very important lesson.

Today, two years after the closing of Carrizo Manuacturing, its 900 former workers are in one of three places: in Piedras Negras, working for other maquiladoras; in the interior of Mexico, struggling to find a job; or in the United States, where they had to emigrate in order to provide for their families, as was recently the case for Juany. At least temporarily, Juany today lives and works somewhere in the middle of Texas.

Many of those who remained in Piedras Negras went to work for Dimmit Industries, a maquiladora making Levi's Dockers. On 28 June 2000, after a series of stoppages, the 1,600 workers at Dimmit forced the union leader (and his supporters in management) to convene a union assembly, where the majority democratically elected a new general secretary for their local. Mixed among the Dimmit workers were the former Carrizo workers, back in action, including Juany and Paty, who were advising the workers from outside the plant.

How Do We Measure Success?

Progressive foundations and agencies for international cooperation would love the grant proposals they receive to include verifiable indicators of achievement and quantitative measures of success. We hear often that funders like visible results, such as the construction of a new irrigation canal, or the reform of a specific law. Sometimes, however, the enormous enterprise of challenging the unbalanced forces of global capitalism is not so tangible or so visible. It is seldom reflected in cyberspace. On a human level, though, such efforts reach deeper into the lives of those who are most affected by the negative impacts of globalization. Positive social change flows from a strengthened sense of dignity and self-respect.

Juany Cázares and Paty Leyva know that will never receive what was withheld from them and their people so dishonourably, but they are proud to have fought as best they could — and that in itself is a great triumph.

Note

1 *Ja, kehre nur der holden Erdensonne*
  Entschlossen deinen Rücken zu!
  Vermesse dich, die Pforten aufzureißen,
  Vor denen jeder gern vorüberschleicht!
  Hier ist es Zeit, durch Taten zu beweisen,
  Das Manneswürde nicht der Götterhöhe wiecht,
  Vor jener dunkeln Höhle nicht zu beben.

Patents and Plants
How Developing Countries Are Protecting Their Genetic Resources

In a world of rapidly integrating markets, the producers of new goods from machines to software are increasingly concerned about protecting the technologies on which their products are based. In many instances, these products required substantial investments that can only be returned through sales and royalty payments. To protect these interests, most governments have enacted intellectual property laws to protect the rights and interests of owners of patents and copyrights. These patents and copyrights can also provide important incentives to create new knowledge in the form of inventions and innovations.

In recent years, major exporters of software, cosmetics, watches, cassette recordings and designer clothing have lost billions of dollars of trade because of violations of copyrights and patents. Counterfeit Gucci handbags, Rolex watches and Microsoft software have been readily available everywhere from street stalls to computer shops throughout the world, and particularly in the Third World. This concern over copyright infringement led to the decision in 1988 to include intellectual property rights in the World Trade Organization (WTO) and the creation of dispute procedures that can lead to punitive retaliation.

As the Uruguay Round negotiations progressed in the early 1990s, however, developing countries became increasingly aware that so-called Trade-Related Intellectual Property Rights (TRIPs) were reaching far beyond the objective of protecting exporters against counterfeiting and uncompensated technology transfer. While protecting investments and providing incentives, patents may also limit the dissemination of important new knowledge and prevent newly industrializing countries from closing the gap with the developed world (early Japanese industrialization, for instance, was to a large degree due to the unrestricted import and use of western technology, while many Asian technologies were freely employed during European industrialization). Patents may also, in the case of genetic resources, enable outsiders to access and control what many developing countries, farmers and indigenous people consider fundamental public goods cared for over many generations.

Today, one of the key issues in patents is that genetic resources used in traditional medicines and found in food crops throughout the developing world are increasingly used in Western pharmaceutical products and foods that are subsequently patented and sold back to developing countries. There are four US patents, for example, on brazzien, a sweet protein found in a berry plant in Gabon, that is now being introduced into fruit and vegetables by US biotechnology companies to obtain products that are sweet but low in calories.

This conflict between the producers of new foods and medicines and the countries where they originally acquired the genetic material sharpened in the 1990s. The debate was nowhere fiercer than within the WTO and specifically around the new TRIPs agreement. The issue boiled down to one of applicability. Could plants and animals – genetic material – be patented? In other words, could genetic material be lumped together with high-definition TV, the latest release from Madonna and a Stephen King bestseller under the general heading of intellectual property rights? And do developing countries facing national emergencies have the right to ignore patents, as Brazil did when it produced and distributed medicines for AIDS sufferers?

Developing countries by and large have not wanted genetic material to be subject to patents. On the other hand, the pharmaceutical and plant-breeding industries, which strongly backed the

TRIPs negotiations, believe that ownership and control of plant genetic resources are a vital element in product development. Given that roughly 80 per cent of plant genetic resources are in developing countries while roughly 80 per cent of biotechnology industries are in developed countries, patent rights are essential to the latter's interests. In short, once a gene is introduced into a product, patent coverage requirements in the WTO would protect its industrial use. The TRIPs agreement would then protect these patents and copyrights internationally.

The bottom line, then, is who controls genetic material: the developing countries or the biotechnology industries? And who determines where this debate takes place and according to what rules? From the perspective of the multinational corporations producing medicines and food, the WTO would be a logical place for the global governance of intellectual property rights. It currently has 144 members, including the recently admitted People's Republic of China. It has a small, efficient, unbureaucratic professional secretariat staff of about 250 lawyers and economists. Its dispute settlement procedures allow one member state to retaliate if another member state does not uphold WTO agreements. What institution other than the WTO could better protect the very considerable proportion of world trade (up to 40 per cent) involving plant genetic resources?

Inside TRIPs

The Trade-Related Intellectual Property Rights treaty (TRIPs), signed into practice in 1995, is an exceptionally arcane piece of international law. It is not a long document – only 32 pages and 71 articles. But it is complex and far-reaching. TRIPs gives extensive intellectual property rights to the owners not only of patents and copyrights, but also of industrial designs, geographic designations ('Champagne', for example) and trademarks. It defines these terms as well as the rights of the holder (the rights of France in the case of champagne, because it comes from the Champagne region of that country), and requires all member states to establish laws to enforce these rights. Implementation of the overall agreement by developing country member governments was reviewed in the WTO TRIPs Council in 2000. Least-developed countries were given an additional five years to implement the agreement.

In terms of the patentability of plants and animals, the debate hinges on a single provision of the TRIPs agreement: Article 27.3(b). Thanks to alert developing country negotiators, Article 27.3(b) of the TRIPs agreement exempts genetic material from being patented. Genetic material in this case is defined as

> plants and animals other than microorganisms, and essentially biological processes for the productions of plants or animals other than non-biological and microbiological processes. However, Members shall provide for the protection of plant varieties either by patents or by an effective *sui generis* system or by any combination thereof.

An enormous amount of wealth and power rides on the interpretation of these two sentences, which form an extraordinarily vague provision in a highly technical and legal trade agreement. On the one hand, in the very vagueness of the language lies the potential for developing countries to use national legislation to sidestep a patent system that largely benefits developed countries. The concept of an 'effective *sui generis* system' of plant variety protection establishes a legal basis for national legislation that would define the genetic resources found in traditional crops and medicines as public goods. The protection does not have to conform to any standards for patents, but it must be effective. On the other hand, the article does not define 'effective'. In other words, the language of Article 27.3(b) does not adequately describe what kinds of legislation can substitute for patents and what kinds can withstand a challenge within the WTO structure.

After the conclusion of the Uruguay Round in 1995, developing countries had four years before the 1999 review in which to enact legislation to protect their genetic resources. When the 1999 review rolled around, the debate on Article 27.3(b) intensified. Some developing countries effectively used the four-year moratorium on implementation to draft and enact legislation (or 'effective *sui generis* systems') that protect their national genetic resources as well as new plant varieties produced in both national and foreign seed-breeding industries. Some of these national laws drew on principles already embodied in the Convention on Biological Diversity (CBD): equitable access to plant genetic resources, appropriate benefit sharing, and the need for 'prior, informed consent' before the exploitation of genetic materials.

For example, in 1998, Costa Rica enacted a law on biodiversity that will serve as a basis for protecting its plant resources. This legislation also includes respect for cultural diversity, namely the cultural practices and knowledge of peasant communities and indigenous peoples. This cultural knowledge is considered tantamount to intellectual property. Under the provisions of this legislation, in other words, a sacred rite of the Cabecar people can no more be copied for commercial purposes than the jingle that Brian Eno composed for Microsoft's Windows operating system. India, the Philippines, Kenya and other countries have enacted or drafted similar *sui generis* plant protection legislation.

Perhaps the most advanced legislation is not national but, rather, regional. In 1996, the Andean Pact countries of Bolivia, Colombia, Ecuador, Peru and Venezuela adopted the Andean Community Common System on Access to Genetic Resources. The Common System recognizes the historical contribution of indigenous communities to biodiversity, its conservation, development and sustainable use, and the benefits provided by such contribution. It acknowledges that the close interdependence between these indigenous communities and biodiversity must be strengthened.

> Customary laws and practices are upheld to the extent that: (a) the rights and decision-making capacities of communities with regard to their knowledge, innovations and practices are recognized and valued, and (b) that communities are free to exchange resources and knowledge among themselves or for their own consumption in accordance with their customary practices.

Under the Common System, any patents on genetic materials obtained outside the Andean Community need not be respected within the Community, thus upholding Article 27.3(b)'s exclusion of genetic materials from patenting.

As a result of this legislation, biotechnology interests in developed countries cannot play one country off against its neighbours. Thus, the Common System gives members sovereign rights over their genetic resources and the right to determine the conditions of access.

The Review Process

Throughout the review process of Article 27.3(b), developing countries pursued three different strategies: to establish firmly the Article's exclusions; to define or redefine its terms in order to expand the exclusions; or to eliminate WTO requirements for plant variety protection altogether. The differences among these three strategies, however, were minor and not a source of contention among developing countries. In their common approach to strengthening the exclusions, rather than diluting them, developing countries showed a remarkable degree of solidarity.

Meanwhile, the United States, the European Union (EU) and other developed countries countered with two strategies of their own. They tried to delete 27.3(b) and with it any exclusions for plant and animal material. Failing this, they sought to replace the ambiguous phrase 'effective *sui generis* system' with the plant protection standards of the Union for the Protection of New

Varieties of Plants (UPOV), to which most developed countries and a few developing countries are parties. UPOV, in its current 1991 version, strengthens the rights of the breeders. Breeders can claim royalties from farmers who plant protected varieties; farmers cannot save seeds for replanting unless government legislation explicitly provides for such; and protected varieties cannot be used for further research without express permission from the breeder. More fundamentally, the criteria used for protection – that the plant variety be 'distinct, uniform and stable' – has raised alarms that these would replace genetically diverse and locally adapted seeds. In other words, the plant gene pool would shrink, and many important natural varieties would disappear.

If Article 27.3(b) is excised from TRIPs, a worst-case scenario supported by the US, extremely broad domestic patent laws that go beyond protecting inventions will cover what 'exists in nature'. Widespread patenting of plants and animals would occur. Advances in biotechnology will further expand the circle of what can be patented. Brazzien is only one example. The less dramatic revision favoured by the EU – the incorporation of UPOV provisions – would serve commercial agriculture by severely limiting the rights of traditional farmers to save and replant seeds without paying royalties. It would also restrict further creative research while supporting commercial breeding interests by limiting what is 'new' and by expanding protection for already existing varieties.

Despite the complexity of the debate, the battle lines could not be clearer. Developing countries used the four-year review period to define Article 27.3(b) more carefully in order to protect their own genetic materials and cultural traditions through national legislation and regional accords. Developed countries have tried to overturn Article 27.3(b) or revise it to the point of ineffectiveness. Arguments over the meaning of Article 27.3(b) in turn generated arguments over the meaning of the review process itself. Developed countries insisted that the review was not a reconsideration of the provision but an assessment of implementation.

Developing countries saw in this an attempt by developed countries to prepare for future challenges to enacted legislation in the WTO dispute settlement body. Whether over the provision itself, the meaning of the review period or at some later date in the dispute settlement procedures of the WTO, the argument has taken different forms but has remained essentially the same. Who controls the genetic material found in plants and animals: indigenous communities, farmers and the national governments of developing countries, or the biotechnology companies and their sponsors among the governments of developed countries?

The NGO Response

A number of NGOs have rallied support for developing country efforts to preserve, if not expand Article 27.3(b) exclusions. Some are campaigning on the slogan 'no patents on life'. Others, especially indigenous peoples and developing country farmer organizations, are lobbying their governments to expand Article 27.3(b) exclusions. Still others are working directly with developing country WTO delegations to support their capacities to resist developed country efforts to shrink exclusion.

Adopting this last approach, the Quaker United Nations Office and Quaker Peace and Service in London published a discussion paper in 1998 on trade, intellectual property, food and biodiversity.[1] Over 10,000 copies were printed in English, French, Spanish and German. This document was widely distributed and read throughout the international trade and environment community. Backed up by a subsequent series of seminars on Article 27.3(b), it helped to provide legal and scientific support to developing country members of the WTO in the review process. The seminars enabled participants to compare national legislation on plant protection in order to assist developing countries still considering or just beginning to draft legislation. In addition, developing country delegations to the WTO were able to better coordinate their strategies in order to present a united front during the review process.[2]

The country representatives and specialists concentrated their attention on three key issues during these discussions: the definition of terms in Article 27.3(b), the compatibility of TRIPs and the CBD, and the creation of effective national legislation. In terms of defining the terms in Article 27.3(b), delegates and experts believed there was considerable scope for interpretation of two key scientific phrases: 'essentially biological' and 'microbiological processes'. The phrase 'essentially biological' is derived from EU law. According to the interpretation of the European Patent Office, 'a process for the production of plants comprising at least one essential technical step, which cannot be carried out without human intervention ... does not fall within the essentially biological exception to patentability'. Thus, a new hybrid variety of corn, created by scientists in the laboratory, could be protected because it is not essentially biological. However, the TRIPs agreement does not support this kind of definition. Rather, according to TRIPs, the genetic modification of plant cells and the regeneration and propagation of plants *are* essentially biological and therefore can be refused patent protection.

The European Patent Office counters this definition by insisting that a technical intervention such as gene splicing must be considered a 'microbiological process'. Such a process, even according to Article 27.3(b), is not 'essentially biological'. However, the language on microbiological process in TRIPs can be interpreted differently. Thus, on another reading, only the initial transformation of the plant cell is treated as microbiological, but the resulting plant (such as the hybrid ear of corn) could not be patented. In other words, the technical process could be patented, but not the plant itself.

The experts concurred that the TRIPs agreement sets minimum standards for patentability. The fact that some innovations have been granted patents in some member states does not imply an obligation for other member states to do the same – bearing in mind the national treatment principle, which requires that foreign and domestic producers be treated the same way. If the US grants a patent to brazzien, Ghana is under no obligation to honour the patent. Ghana could exempt brazzien from patentability and, by virtue of national legislation, declare the sweet protein a national resource that can be used freely by any Ghanaian. In effect, members can have broader standards if they want, or they can have minimum standards. Ultimately, a Dispute Settlement Panel will have to decide what these words mean.

There was general agreement that TRIPs and the CBD need to be more compatible and mutually supportive. As it stands, the two agreements could be seen as serving different objectives on the issue of access to natural resources. The CBD establishes the sovereign right of states to their own natural resources and their right to require prior informed consent before any of these resources can be extracted. TRIPs, on the other hand, allows exclusion from patenting on plants and animals (though not for micro-organisms) and thereby allows for genetic resources to remain a public good, not subject to any rights, even of sovereign governments.

The CBD, in other words, strengthens the right of governments to protect genetic resources from commercial exploitation while the TRIPs agreement gives more weight to non-restrictive access. CBD serves developing country interests, as the examples of national legislation incorporating the basic CBD principles clearly illustrate. Further strengthening such legislation, the CBD is designed to facilitate access to and transfer of 'technologies that are relevant to the conservation and sustainable use of biological diversity'. It also requires contracting parties to ensure that patents and intellectual property rights support CBD objectives.

Can WTO member states invoke the the CBD to justify measures that are contrary to TRIPs? Neither agreement addresses this contingency. However, as long as exclusions in Article

27.3(b) remain broad, they may help limit the potentially negative effects of patents on the objectives of CBD – technology transfer, sustainable use, or the equitable sharing of benefits. It is unclear how a WTO Dispute Settlement Panel would rule if one government uses TRIPs to gain access to a plant's genetic material that another government is trying to protect using the CBD. On the one hand, the TRIPs agreement, because it was the later of the two treaties, would take priority under international law. On the other hand, priority could be given to the CBD, given the exclusions in 27.3(b) and the greater specificity in the CBD.

In terms of national legislation (*sui generis* systems), India has been a trailblazer. Indian legislation emphasizes the rights of farmers, village communities and researchers, provides a measure of protection for different species and varieties of plants, and encourages the sustainable development of agricultural biodiversity. The legislation is currently in a parliamentary committee. If enacted, it will stimulate investments for research and development. It will also facilitate the growth of the domestic seed industry, which will ensure the availability of high-quality seeds and improved varieties for farmers. The legislation includes compulsory licensing and CBD benefit-sharing arrangements.

From the Indian case and other examples, four criteria for effective legislation can be identified. Legislation should (1) serve the national interest; (2) provide a balance between plant breeders' rights and farmers' and researchers' rights; (3) protect the varieties that breeders register with the authorities; and (4) require prior authorization of the breeder for further use. Given the current flexibility of 27.3(b), these criteria would enable governments to ignore the more stringent requirements placed on commercial agriculture by, for example, the European Union.

The more these criteria are incorporated in legislation, the greater the prospects that challenges in the WTO mounted by developed countries will fail. In addition, the more legislation is enacted by developing countries, the more difficult it will be for a panel to rule against these for failing to abide by TRIPs requirements.

Looking Ahead

So far, developing countries have achieved some overall success in the WTO in preserving the basic provisions of 27.3(b). A few countries, such as India, argue that exclusions under 27.3(b) should be broadened, at least as a bargaining chip for future negotiations. In the meantime, developing countries are creating facts on the ground through effective legislation that enshrines biological diversity as a national or regional goal. Whether through international negotiations on the language of the TRIPs agreement or in the realm of national legislation, developing countries are successfully preventing biotechnology industries from using patents to own and control precious genetic resources.

Assuming that developing countries can hold their ground, this success is indicative of a much greater resistance on the part of developing countries in the WTO. In the Uruguay Round, developed countries' negotiating tactics burdened developing countries with more implementation obligations than they could meet. The demands of developing countries for fewer obligations and longer implementation timeframes, more than any other factor, blocked the plan of developed countries to start a new multilateral trade round at the WTO Seattle Conference. This is good news because it reflects the growing strength of developing countries in the WTO.

The other good news is that the Article 27.3(b) review demonstrates the growing determination and enhanced negotiating skills of developing countries as they protect their interests in the world trading system. The debate on who controls plant and animal resources has also thrown a spotlight on how much the patent system favours developed countries at the expense of the rest of the WTO's members. The arguments are complex, but the alternatives are clear. Costa Rica, India, and other developing countries, in protecting their own biological and cultural diversity, are leading the way to a more equitable world trade system.

Notes

1 Geoff Tansey, *Trade, Intellectual Property, Food and Biodiversity: Key Issues and Options for the 1999 Review of Article 27.3(b) of the TRIPs Agreement*, London: Quaker Peace and Service, 1999.

2 The most recent meeting in September 1999 addressed TRIPs Article 27.3(b), definitions, CBD compatibility and *sui generis* systems. Twenty-two developing country delegations to the WTO met for two days with legal and scientific experts from the Kenya Industrial Property Office, the Indian Ministry of Agriculture and Cooperation, the Guatemalan Ministry of Economy, Thailand's Department of Agriculture and the Ecuadorian Ministry of Agriculture. Previous seminars brought together similar experts from South Africa, Philippines, Egypt and Peru.

Constructing
Economic Solidarity
COMAL in Honduras

Mary McCann Sánchez

In 1994, the Portillo family was completely discouraged. Small-scale farmers who had emigrated from central to western Honduras and successfully acquired a small plot of arable land during the period of agrarian reform, the Portillos had diversified from corn and bean production into the production of rice. However, drought and the importation of rice in the mid-1990s provoked a crisis for local producers, despite the fact that the demand for rice continued to be high. News of 'free trade' policies and promises of future riches were in the air, but the Portillo family and other farmers in their community felt trapped by the potential loss of their livelihood.

As the forces of globalization sweep through Central America, rural poor like the Portillos have been perhaps the hardest-hit sector of the population. They have watched as the goods they produce fall in value with the lowering of trade barriers and the influx of imports. But the rural poor are not giving up. By establishing a regional trade system in Honduras, rural producers and consumers have found that solidarity can have very practical economic benefits.

From War to Economic Integration

In the 1970s and 1980s, the isthmus of Central America was a focal point of international attention and debate. A tropical area which enjoyed relatively limited economic interaction with the outside world, Central America was best known for its export of high-quality raw materials – coffee, bananas, wood and minerals – and for the wars that tore through three of the five countries in the region. As El Salvador and Guatemala moved into prolonged warfare, in 1979 Nicaragua's rebel forces won a military victory. Peace was short-lived as the new government confronted severe economic restrictions and a Contra war. Honduras, in the geographic centre, became the temporary home of refugees from its three neighbours and simultaneously a base for regional intervention by the United States. In the south of the isthmus, Costa Rica passed through a less volatile period marked by a significantly higher standard of living and the lack of military forces. Panama, not included in the five stars of Central American history but with growing economic and ideological ties, entered a critical time of definition of national sovereignty.

It was a tense and intense period. The cost of the wars was high in terms of land control, use of natural resources and rising poverty. Outside analysts commented that Central America had become the field upon which the Cold War would play out its final engagement. Inside interpretations addressed the urgency of the struggle for survival at a time when violations of human rights were commonplace, ideological barriers seemingly impenetrable and the most normal activities, such as planting, harvesting and marketing crops, were high-risk activities in conflict zones and across national borders.

At the outset of the 1990s, the peace processes in El Salvador and Guatemala advanced due to a convergence of internal and external factors: the human and economic costs of the war were high and less defensible on all fronts; the East–West balance had changed; and the region was falling behind the pace of a rapidly changing world. Central America entered a new phase of negotiated settlements at the national level and renewed efforts for regional integration.

There was effervescence – combined with a sense of wariness – at this historic juncture. Demilitarization and the opening of democratic spaces were victories for a broad spectrum of Central American civil society. Many civic groups hoped that the growing acceptance of human rights would lead to a broader understanding of economic rights and respect for the environment. While the Peace Accords signed in El Salvador in 1992 did not attempt to resolve either economic inequities or social disparities, the example of negotiated settlements could serve as a model for dialogue and increased citizen participation. At the same time, these hopes were tempered by tough realities in the region: the continuing dependence on authoritarian models, the proliferation of small arms, increasing street violence, high levels of unemployment, and serious problems of internal and external debt in Honduras and Nicaragua. [1]

The end of armed struggle in the region also meant the beginning of greater engagement with globalization. Foreign investors looked to Central America as a new site for the operation of the drawback industry, commonly known in the region as the 'maquila'. In the case of Honduras, the export of non-traditional products such as shrimp, lobster, palm oil and textiles produced in maquila factories began to take on greater significance in the 1990s, representing 55 per cent of total exports in a country where traditional exports had amounted to 78 per cent of total exports.[2] Economic restructuring programmes, generally called 'structural adjustment programmes', were aimed at reducing public expenditures, privatizing enterprises controlled by the state, and establishing a 'free market' system. According to the Comisión Económica para América Latina y el Caribe (CEPAL), Honduras registered an average of 3.7 per cent growth in its gross national product in 1991–7.[3] This compared favourably with a low GNP growth rate of 0.7 from 1980 to 1984, but was significantly less than the growth rate of 8.8 per cent recorded by the GNP in the late 1970s.[4]

The economic changes of the 1990s, moreover, tended to favour portions of society with access to the latest technology, leaving behind large sectors of the population. In the case of

Honduras, the situation of small-scale rural producers was particularly troubling: in 1994, CEPAL reported that 76 per cent of the rural population lived below the poverty line, with 55 per cent considered indigent.[5] Globalization brought to rural producers, known as *campesinos*, intense competition from products such as imported basic grains from developed countries as well as the marketing of products previously unknown to the new consumer market. At the same time that rural producers faced the challenges of the market, they experienced difficulties as consumers. The consumer price index quickly rose from 100.0 in 1990 to 196.4 in 1996.[6] Hondurans experienced the highest price hikes in Central America, with the steady devaluation of Honduran currency, the *Lempira*, making the situation even more acute. The cost of a weekly shopping basket, the *canasta básica*, rose approximately 20 per cent annually. In 1997, Honduras ranked 116 out of 174 countries in the United Nations Human Development Index, in comparison with 80 in 1990 and 101 in 1992.[7]

The Search for Alternatives

It was in this context that the American Friends Service Committee began to work with rural people in Honduras to search for *alternativas económicas*. Convinced that the chronic poverty they experienced would not be mitigated by a process of globalization in which Honduras continued to use raw materials and cheap labour to attract foreign investments, organizations of small-scale farmers, farmworkers and rural women's associations called for economic development to enhance human capabilities as well as raise productivity and income. Of particular concern was the inability of small-scale farmers to market their products successfully.

The rural population in Honduras is varied. Of agricultural producers, 19.7 per cent are considered *precaristas*, landless farm labourers who work for a daily wage or rent land for their own production. Their returns are limited and the majority live in conditions of extreme poverty. A further 42 per cent are poor farmers with small plots of land or who produce on national or community land. Despite the fact that their income is low and they lack access to credit, these farmers make a major contribution to food security in the country, producing approximately 40 per cent of the beans and corn grown in Honduras. Then there are the *campesino-finqueros* (27.3 per cent), small-scale farmers with greater stability, potential for growth and diversified crops. These three groups play an important role in providing the staples consumed by the population: their combined production represents 85 per cent of the beans and 79 per cent of the corn produced in Honduras. Farmers organized in cooperatives account for 4.6 per cent of the agricultural population, while 6 per cent are large-scale ranchers and agro-business farmers.[8]

Farming in Honduras, particularly among the poor, continues to be a family enterprise with significant but unremunerated contributions made by women, children and the elderly who work on a daily basis to get water, maintain infrastructure, take care of domestic animals, and seasonally market the family's produce, in addition to sometimes taking part in the traditional activities of planting and harvesting. As the globalization process brought more textile factories to Honduras via the maquila, young rural women have found a new role in supplementing the family economy by emigrating to the export-processing zones and sending remittances back to the rural areas. In a parallel trend, rural youth – both male and female – are increasingly emigrating to the United States with the intention of bolstering the home economy.

A first step in our efforts was to provide a series of opportunities for community-based organizations, farmworkers' associations, rural women's organizations and cooperatives and rural enterprises to analyse their problems. Participation in these regional meetings was diverse in terms of geography and historical experiences: *campesinos* who had organized during the period of agrarian reform (1960s–80s) and had acquired land; women who had emigrated to the northern coast in search of employment with the banana companies and instead had become farm labourers or spouses of farm labourers; indigenous producers of potatoes and basic grains; producers of sugar cane with limited access to the transformation of their product; artisans and craftspersons; and organic producers with difficulties in competing with agro-industry.

The discussions at these meetings repeatedly drew attention to two factors:

- Organizations lacked information on how 'the market' works, despite the fact that 'the market' was being held up not only as the basis of the economy but as a regulator of society itself. In the traditional market process in Honduras intermediaries played a larger than usual role and had not offered a fair framework to small-scale producers. At the same time, the global market set up significant barriers blocking access for rural people to information, communication and capital.

- To enter the market as a serious player or to create alternative processes, greater strength was imperative. That strength would necessarily be based both on greater volume of products to be marketed and on a greater capacity to take on new economic, social and political roles.

The common thread in the discussion was rural people's marked exclusion from economic decisions and processes on a practical, business level as well as on the policy level. At the level of testimonials, the exchange was powerful. Members of rice cooperatives recounted that before organizing a cooperative effort, their only contact with the market was via intermediaries, or *coyotes* as they are sometimes termed, who also served as moneylenders to farmers unable to acquire credit in banks, thus maintaining a firm control over the financial situation of the producer. Independent farmers in the central valley, seeking to diversify with cash crops, experienced excessive losses by selling onions at prices far below the market price in the major cities because they had no access to reliable price information. Farmers throughout the country cited the problem of weights and measurements, with intermediaries using gunny sacks, termed *costales*, rather than weighing products. Though producers were certain that they were losing up to 20 per cent of the value of their product in this system, they had no means to counter the trend.

The problems were also reflected in the people's identities as consumers. A group of eight women from *precarista* families in central Honduras shared their concerns about the availability of food and the need to establish a small food store in a remote community abandoned by both government and private enterprise. Maintaining a balanced diet in rural areas is very difficult where poor roadways and lack of transportation ensure high prices for non-local products. Throughout the discussions, the perception that food security and the interests of poor consumers were not priorities in a free market agenda was widely shared.

The sense of exclusion, however, was not defeatist by any means. Complemented by a powerful desire to '*crear espacio*', or find openings, organizations participating in the initial consultations proposed ways of responding to the felt crisis and breaking the isolation through economic solidarity.

The Birth of COMAL

In 1995, a clear-cut project emerged. Small-scale agricultural producers in Honduras, organized in cooperatives, church-based organizations, women's organizations and farmworkers' associations, proposed to transform their local economies via active and sustainable commercial relations. In the absence of a market system that could provide a decent livelihood to the producer and render a fair price to consumers, a network of social organizations from the productive sector would market basic grains and staple items of daily consumption to rural and marginalized urban communities.

The idea took on a name, the Alternative Community Trade Network (COMAL). A *comal* is a traditional cooking instrument found throughout Central America, round in shape and usually handmade from natural clay. The *comal* is placed, like a skillet, over an open fire or stove to cook corn tortillas, a staple in most Central American cultures. The choice of the *comal* as symbol became a reaffirmation of food security at the most basic level, of both men and women's contributions to economic livelihood, and of the endurance of cultures and traditions at risk.

COMAL had an ambitious agenda: to ensure that local organizations could effectively coordinate actions to achieve the volume needed to become economic and political players. Community stores, already established by many organizations on a small scale and in sometimes isolated locations, would benefit from quality products at better prices and access to greater technical skills and as such could better serve low-income populations. The initiative was highly grassroots-oriented, with a strong commitment from the American Friends Service Committee (AFSC) to support organization, assist in building an administrative and legal base, form a technical team and accompany a complex process of building bridges across sectors and borders. Four initial programmes developed in planned phases: Education and Training, Price Information System, Marketing and Institution Building.

At the organizational level, one of the first steps was to establish the values of the network. With the participation of twelve founding member organizations, the Alternative Marketing Network established its business principles:

- Prioritization of work and participation over capital;

- Fair prices and true commodities in all marketing transactions;

- Transparency in financial transactions;

- Unity through a faith in transformation;

- Justice and solidarity in practice;

- Respect for each person and the equality of rights without regard to differences of gender, race, religion, or ideology;

- Honesty and honour in practice;

- Respect for life and for nature.

COMAL put together a Board of Directors and a Representative Assembly and created a strategic map that would guide the process in the first six years. Both the Board and the Representative Assembly are formed by representatives of the member organizations, reflecting the commitment of COMAL to a process of governance built from the bottom up.

Programmatically, the Education and Training Programme was the point of departure. The exclusion of small-scale rural producers and farmworkers from decision making in the market is closely related to the endemic lack of basic education for the poor and to low literacy rates, especially among women. COMAL embarked upon a rigorous schedule of training in organization, marketing, administration, and gender in community economics. One condition of membership in the network was participation in training sessions.

Because it was a network, not a new organization, COMAL could draw on a wealth of human resources as well as the complexity of diverse backgrounds and ideologies. From within the member organizations, experienced 'popular educators' with skills strengthened in literacy programmes, religion-based communities, health brigades and farmworker movements took on the challenge and trained local people to become multipliers of knowledge in the areas of administration, accounting, marketing

and simple economics. Young people were encouraged to participate, and COMAL actively sought opportunities for youth
education and advancement. COMAL developed a team of
internal auditors to monitor member stores on a monthly basis,
thus complementing the efforts of professional accountants who
would evaluate overall administration.

The Education Programme also assumed the important task
of transmitting the principles of the COMAL network to
organizations interested in becoming part of the network and in
continuing to facilitate the kinds of exchanges so important at the
outset of the process. A critical task has been to promote geographically based regional coordination of member organizations.
The commitment to a process of personal and social transformation,
in line with Freirean principles and practice,[9] meant that education
on a technical level should also promote analysis and self-
evaluation. The particular challenge of COMAL was to ensure
that the technical training would be rigorous and would promote
the efficiency needed while at the same time encouraging participants to be active subjects in the process.

The Price Information System responded to the concern that
vulnerability and exploitation are related to a lack of information.
As the network grew from 20 to 36 organizations in the period
1995–9, COMAL recognized its potential to transmit information
on price trends in a timely and efficient manner. By organizing
and training a group of 21 information monitors who gather
market information on a weekly basis, COMAL produces a
weekly price sheet of 30 basic items of consumption. The
information is used by local organizations to facilitate business
transactions with other organizations and to advise local producers
who traditionally have sold their products at distorted prices.
Through this Price Information System, COMAL works to
improve the negotiating capacity of its members in hopes of later
moving into negotiating policy at multisectoral and governmental
levels.

In a globalized world, information is often called 'the name of the game'. Agility in moving information around and making timely decisions is of paramount importance. Rural Honduras presents clear examples of just how uneven the playing field is in terms of communication. In 1997 there were 14 telephones per 1,000 inhabitants in Honduras, in contrast with 195 in Costa Rica[10] and 681 per 1,000 in Sweden.[11] The urgency of making information accessible meant taking preliminary steps in acquiring basic technology and training people in its use, actions which COMAL prioritized in 1997 and 1998. The thrust of the Information System is to enable local producers and consumers to negotiate and to make quicker yet solidly based financial decisions, a trend similar to the aspirations of many financial institutions throughout the industrialized, globalized world. Yet, at the same time, COMAL recognizes that information is useful only to the extent that human beings are qualified and confident in its collection, interpretation and application. And, counter to a strictly financial motivation, COMAL encourages a high level of consultation and consensus among member organizations, despite the demands of quick answers and actions, in order to respect the basic principle of human and economic solidarity.

An Alternative Market

The commercial activity itself, the Marketing Programme, commenced in mid-1998 when COMAL had accumulated a base of capital from membership dues, contributions and grants from international organizations. The Marketing Programme buys and sells basic grains within the network, via its centre of operations, a central warehouse and 36 regional centres. It also purchases more than 40 kinds of products such as cooking oil, salt, soap, sugar and farming tools from national industries for distribution in 500 community stores across the country. The stores themselves are initiatives of the member organizations. In order to be affiliated with the COMAL network, personnel at the stores undergo training as described above.

Eight regional committees, comprised of representatives of member organizations, supervise the marketing activities across the country. COMAL strives to have a decentralized model in order to promote participation and local responsibility. Regional warehouses and locally based administrators play an important role. The goal of the marketing activity is to make basic goods available at a reasonable cost and to generate economic activity and employment in the rural areas. The volume of sales has grown significantly in just over two years. By the end of the year 2000, sales levels reached US$989,000. The demand for expanding operations is high. Projections for the future include greater emphasis on agricultural products, herbal medicines and traditional handicrafts.

An important financial aspect is the *Fondo Colectivo* (Common Fund) formed by the capital of member organizations. When an organization affiliates with the COMAL network, it makes a deposit in the Common Fund, a deposit that accrues interest. The member organization has the right to acquire products sold through the network on a credit basis because of its participation in the fund, currently set as a credit of 200 per cent of its original deposit for a period of ten days. This ensures that the community stores can make timely purchases while at the same time promoting the necessary efficiency in sales, stock and bookkeeping. Most importantly, contributing to the fund inculcates a sense of ownership in the enterprise.

At the outset of the year 2000, COMAL subdivided its Marketing Programme into two areas: the Family Basket and *Producto Campesino* (Farmers' Products). The Family Basket makes basic subsistence items available to the community stores and is a direct link between industry and the consumers, thus making basic necessities available at lower prices. *Producto Campesino* takes on the challenge of locating markets and facilitating sales for member organizations who produce basic grains, sugar cane, cacao, potatoes and eggs, an essential task if small-scale farmers are not only to survive, but to flourish. According to COMAL affiliates organized in cooperatives as rice producers, the stranglehold that middlemen have traditionally exerted on its membership has been significantly modified because of organization at a local level and participation in national networks. The programme also examines the possibility of creating, via appropriate technology and other means, agro-industrial centres for adding value to local products for consumption, so that the producers will enjoy a higher margin of profit.

The Network has the experience of a simple but very effective process of technology transfer with cane producers in Ecuador and Colombia, affiliates of Maquita Cushunchic and RELACC (Latin American Alternative Community Marketing Network), who trained Honduran sugar cane producers in the production of *panela granulada*, an organic brown sugar with a higher nutrient composition than refined white sugar. The Honduran producers, in turn, transferred the technology to growers in neighbouring El Salvador: in both countries the product is being marketed on a small scale within the alternative marketing networks affiliated to RELACC. The importance of the product is not only economic: there are significant ecological advantages. Sugar cane producers in Central America have traditionally engaged in dangerous environmental practices, such as burning rubber tyres in open stoves, an inordinate use of chemical fertilizers, and the depletion of nutrients in the soil. The introduction of alternative products that generate greater income for the local producer allows these practices to be revised or abandoned. Affiliates of COMAL have achieved organic certification and comply with health and quality-control standards, all necessary steps in a process of sustainable development.

Through the Marketing Programme, approximately 14,000 rural families have made modest economic gains in their buying power as consumers. The system of community stores boosts employment at the local level, generates income for its affiliates, and creates social funds that are managed locally and substitute for the missing safety net in Honduras. The success of the community stores has instilled a new sense of hope in rural areas. At the regional and national level, the challenge is to reach a break-even point, in which each centre has the necessary infrastructure to operate as a sustainable, profitable enterprise that can take its place in the private sector and simultaneously serve the population it represents.

Branching Out

The ongoing Institution Building component of COMAL works in the areas of management, administration and financial planning to ensure the consolidation and longevity of the endeavour. Part of the task of that department was to gain legal status for COMAL, based on its internal statutes and its role within Honduran society. The legal status, or *personería jurídica*, was achieved at the beginning of 2000. Developing the mission, goals and statutes of COMAL with the participation of diverse members, all with different philosophies and social and ethnic compositions, represents an important social contract.

A significant part of Institution Building within COMAL is the combination in each department of university-trained professionals with experience-trained community/organization members, who share the conviction that class divisions so closely tied to the years of violence can be transformed by mutual respect and that new relationships will arise from day-to-day cooperation. At the same time, COMAL maintains the conviction that each team member has a contribution to make and a wisdom born of his or her roots. This translates concretely into a mentorship programme in which specialists in marketing, in agriculture, in economics and in business administration provide ongoing training to counterparts from the member organizations. Due to the inequities that have traditionally existed within Honduras and the problem of corruption at many levels, the challenge is not a mere transmission of practice but the creation and strengthening of truly fair practices which run contrary to the *status quo* and which keep the human person at the centre.

COMAL depends on the persistence of its membership in using their skills to exert their rights as political actors. In the late 1990s, 16 *campesino* enterprise members of COMAL, representing 300 families of rice producers, achieved an important political victory with positive economic ramifications by obtaining direct participation in a national commission making decisions on the import of rice. COMAL forms part of the intersectorial forum Interforos, which promotes the participation of civil society in national development.

The notion of forming alliances of economic solidarity and of building an enterprise based on the strengths, convictions and endurance of the rural poor was not limited to Honduras. It found echo in efforts throughout Latin America – recently joining together via RELACC, based in Quito, Ecuador – and in partic- ular in its founding member, Maquita Cushunchic ('Marketing as Brothers and Sisters' in the Quechua language). Annual meetings with RELACC and participation in training programmes on both a bilateral and a hemispheric basis provided a sense of inspiration and conviction, as well as a set of methodological tools that were critical in the initial stages.

Maintaining its identity as part of RELACC continues to be an important pillar for COMAL. In an effort to promote greater regional integration and open alternative marketing processes across borders, COMAL works with the Mayan Network of Community Marketing (REMACC) in Guatemala, in El Salvador via the National Network of Alternative Marketing (RENACES), and in Nicaragua via the Nicaraguan Network of Community Marketing (RENICC). Though considerable work remains to be done in terms of consolidating national efforts and in playing a greater role in regional policy around integration issues, RELACC has taken initial steps in marketing products across borders via regional farmers' markets, in addition to three exchange visits and working meetings per year.

A constant imperative for COMAL and its counterparts in RELACC is to maintain a principled approach to business and an integral vision of development. The vulnerability of Central America was made clear in late 1998 in the devastation wrought by Hurricane Mitch, exacerbated by ecological degradation and historical patterns of human exploitation. If there are to be effective strategies to eradicate poverty in the region, it is clear that they must address relationships of power, including access to the economic power needed for building a decent livelihood. Both the needs and the potential of the people who make up a society – and their ability and incentive to interact positively with the environment, with technology and with other societies – can provide important signposts to a better existence.

Notes

1 By 1998, the external debt, to bilateral and multilateral lenders, was US$3,824,700,000, according to statistics from the Honduras Secretary of Finances.

2 UNDP, *Human Development Report, Honduras 1999* (Tegucigalpa, Honduras: UNDP, 1999), p. 136.

3 *Ibid.*

4 Hugo Noe Pino, 'The Structural Roots of Crisis: Economic Growth and Decline in Honduras 1950–1984', PhD dissertation, University of Texas at Austin, 1988, p. 160.

5 UNDP, *State of the Region in Human Sustainable Development, Central America, Report No. 1* (San José, Costa Rica: UNDP/EU, 1999), p. 176.

6 UNDP, *State of the Region in Human Sustainable Development, Central America, Report No. 2* (San José, Costa Rica: UNDP/EU, 1999), p. 45.

7 UNDP, *State of the Region in Human Sustainable Development, Central America,*

Report No. 1 (San José, Costa Rica: UNDP/EU, 1999), p. 457.

8 UNDP, *Human Development Report, Honduras 1998* (Tegucigalpa, Honduras: UNDP, 1998), p. 91. The statistics analysed by the UNDP are taken from the Dirección General de Estadística y Censos (DGEC), *Censo Nacional Agropecuario*, 1993.

9 Paulo Freire was an important Brazilian educator whose writing and practice on non-formal education of adults had an impact throughout Latin America, particularly in the 1970s. He is best known for creating a methodology of combining literacy for adults with social analysis.

10 UNDP, *State of the Region in Human Sustainable Development, Central America, Report No. 1* (San José, Costa Rica: UNDP/EU, 1999), p. 147, Chart 5.10. Statistics taken from *Honduras en Cifras 1994–96* (Tegucigalpa).

11 UNDP, *Human Development Report 1998* (New York: UNDP, 1998).

Sowing Seeds of Change
in Bosnia-Herzegovina

James Whooley

Despite the hardships of life in Bosnia-Herzegovina, community activists throughout the country have begun to develop positive responses to the changes brought on by the 1992–5 war and its aftermath. Local non-government organizations have sprung up across the country, helping communities to confront a radically changed political, economic and social landscape. One such organization, the Community Gardening Association (CGA) of Bosnia-Herzegovina, provides opportunities for poor families to grow their own food while facilitating positive cross-cultural contact. Established by the American Friends Service Committee (AFSC) as a response to post-war poverty and ethnic division, the CGA addresses social challenges that are likely to intensify as the impact of globalization increases in Bosnia-Herzegovina in the coming years.

Bosnia-Herzegovina is an occupied country. Through the Office of the High Representative, a supervisory institution established under the Dayton Peace Agreement of 1995, the international community wields considerable power over the country's governance. Various UN agencies pursue reconstruction and peace-building work. Some 20,000 troops from more than 30 countries enforce a still-fragile peace. European institutions set membership standards and fund a variety of programmes. The World Bank and the International Monetary Fund provide loans. Outside countries, particularly those contributing peacekeeping troops and aid money, exert diplomatic and economic influence. International businesses set prerequisites for investment.

International non-government organizations run projects of various sizes and stripes. Together, these various external actors push the leadership of Bosnia-Herzegovina to dismantle the structural remnants of the Yugoslav socialist system and replace them with a market economy and a democratic political system characterized by transparent governance and the rule of law.

This nation-building effort follows on a brutal civil war which between 1992 and 1995 left some quarter of a million people dead and displaced over two million. Recovery from this conflict, which followed Bosnia-Herzegovina's secession from Yugoslavia, has been painfully slow. In politics, the legacy of the war is apparent in the ascendancy of nationalist parties stained by corruption and inefficiency. The ravages of war still cripple the economy, with a damaged industrial and transportation base and a still unsettled population. The country's society and culture remain stunted and fragmented as a result of the war's ethno-religious dividing lines. The changes wrought by the war have been compounded by the scrapping of a socialist system which, while denying many political and civil rights, provided a comprehensive social support system. In the new Bosnia-Herzegovina, housing, education, health care and work are no longer guaranteed by the state, though a minimal, and by all accounts inadequate, welfare system remains.

In this post-conflict environment, it is a matter of semantics as to where 'peace building' ends and 'globalization' begins. For most citizens, globalization – in the form of closer ties to institutional Europe and increased international trade – is less a daily reality than a vague promise of enhanced security, democracy and prosperity. Yet many of the post-war, post-socialism challenges currently facing Bosnia-Herzegovina are issues that also tend to arise in the context of lowered trade barriers, internationalization of local markets, increased capital and labour mobility, and diminished social guarantees – the hallmarks of globalization.

As such, the experience of local projects responding to poverty and urbanization, fragmentation of traditional economic and family structures, and greater socio-economic inequalities will likely prove invaluable as globalization increasingly affects the country. Moreover, the experience of grassroots organizing will empower communities as they confront corruption, a common challenge in societies undergoing globalization-related transitions, and arguably the most severe problem affecting Bosnia-Herzegovina today.

One such local project is quietly operating on the outskirts of Sarajevo, providing food and opportunities for self-help and reconciliation to people whose lives have been upended by the changes of recent years. The experiences of the CGA of Bosnia-Herzegovina demonstrate how the challenges of post-war recovery – and increasingly, globalization – can be met by dedicated and talented individuals working in the context of a well-organized community organization.

The CGA, a project of the American Friends Service Committee, currently operates two gardens in the Sarajevo area – one within the boundaries of the Bosnian-Croat Federation, the other in Republika Srpska. Each garden is divided into plots of around 200 square metres which are allocated to a multi-ethnic participant group identified through local humanitarian organizations. Some 35 families currently tend plots at the two gardens. Two staff agronomists supervise day-to-day operations, oversee the maintenance of the land and water delivery, prepare seedlings in a small greenhouse, and purchase needed tools and seeds. Participants are given advice and guidance as needed, but are expected to do all work necessary to cultivate their vegetables.

The primary goal of the CGA is to provide opportunities for needy urban families to grow and harvest their own food in a multi-ethnic setting. The experience of the first garden in the 2000 growing season demonstrated that this challenge could indeed be met. Despite an unusually hot and dry summer, each family harvested approximately 1100 DM worth of food.

Moreover, relationships among participants were uniformly positive, regardless of ethnicity, and many participants claimed emotional and psychological benefits from the work.

In addition to these individual benefits, the CGA is poised to have a broader impact, addressing at least four issues likely to challenge Bosnia-Herzegovina as it continues its transition to a market-based economy, rule of law and democracy in the coming years: urban poverty and food insecurity, inter-ethnic relations, environmental policy and governance.

Urban Poverty and Food Insecurity

Poverty is a severe problem in Bosnia-Herzegovina. Unemployment tops 50 per cent, and while a government assistance programme for the unemployed is in place, '(p)ractice has shown that these funds are not sufficient to cover the basic cost of living'.[1] At the same time, the traditional safety nets offered by family and community networks have been greatly weakened as a result of the war. Two million people, half the country's population, were internally displaced or made refugees during the war. Fewer than 200,000 of these people have returned to their homes, while more than half a million remain internally displaced.[2]

For many of the participants in the first garden, the value of the vegetables harvested from their small plot during the summer and early fall of 2000 exceeded the amount they received in pension payments for the entire year. The potatoes, tomatoes, cabbage, carrots and onions that could not be immediately consumed or distributed among family and neighbours were jarred in the autumn, using stoves, oil and jarring solution provided by the CGA. In this way the garden provided a partial but year-round source of food for these vulnerable families.

Selection of participants was made with the help of local humanitarian organizations which provided lists of willing participants. CGA staff made the final selection from this pool of applicants based on the criteria of food insecurity, ability to work a plot of land and willingness to work within an ethnically diverse participant group. Hundreds of families expressed interest in joining the project, a sobering indication of the extent to which food insecurity affects the local population, but an encouraging sign of openness to cross-group interaction after almost ten years of ethnic division and recrimination.

The vast majority of garden participants were older adults. Some of these were couples whose adult children were living elsewhere; some were older members of large families living in difficult conditions in the Sarajevo area. In all cases, the war and change of systems had severed or greatly weakened the networks that would have supported these older adults.

Older adults are among the more vulnerable groups in Bosnia-Herzegovina in this time of upheaval and transition. Migration and unemployment have weakened family support networks even as the loss of state services and reduction of pensions have made older adults more dependent on informal assistance. The experience of many older adults in countries undergoing the first effects of lowered trade barriers and diminished social guarantees is similar. This suggests that the experience of the garden in providing seniors with an opportunity to be active and productive may well prove relevant as globalization begins to change Bosnia-Herzegovina in the coming years. Migration will increase as young people continue to seek work opportunities beyond their own borders, while the quest for macro-economic health will likely prevent any significant improvement in state social guarantees in the short to medium term.[3]

The CGA reaches out to at least two other vulnerable groups: ethnic minorities and women. In the aftermath of a bitter war, those who are not members of the majority group in a particular area face many difficulties. The Organization for Security and Cooperation in Europe has reported widespread employment discrimination, denial of utility services, police protection, health, education, pensions and other public goods, and numerous instances of violence and intimidation against minorities.[4] Yet minority returns continue to increase, indicating that diversity will once again be the reality in much of Bosnia-Herzegovina, especially in urban areas. These returnees face the double challenge of a moribund economy and ethnic discrimination in securing enough food for themselves and their dependents. By reaching out to members of these groups, the CGA offers a chance to augment family food supplies as well as an opportunity to be involved in a community organization dedicated to tolerance and respect.

As with minorities, women are underrepresented in the workforce and in government, though there have been recent signs of progress in this regard.[5] This inequality is especially problematic for female-headed households faced with job-market as well as child-care obstacles. The CGA offers an opportunity for work while also providing a space for children. Several of the participants at the first garden brought their grandchildren with them, thus allowing the mothers of these children to work. Activities for the children included giving each a small plant to care for and providing games and books. As with older adults, women will face special challenges as Bosnia-Herzegovina continues its transition to an internationally oriented, market economy. Traditional child care arrangements will no longer suffice as women increasingly enter the workforce, and discrimination will likely remain a problem. By identifying women as a vulnerable group within its mandate for service, the CGA will call attention to the situation of women and provide opportunities for participants looking to overcome these obstacles.

In addition to fragmenting family and community networks, migration has contributed to food insecurity by virtue of increased urbanization. During the war urban centres swelled with displaced persons, some from other cities but many from rural areas, seeking protection and material aid. In the war's aftermath, many rural–

urban migrants are electing to stay in the cities, where jobs, education and social services are more accessible. This pattern of urbanization matches that of other countries undergoing economic and social transitions associated with neo-liberal development and globalization. Indeed, 90 per cent of the developing world's population growth is projected to take place within cities in the next twenty years. Both the World Bank and the United Nations Development Programme have predicted that this trend will be accompanied by massive increases in urban poverty.[6] Food insecurity related to this poverty is especially threatening given that urbanites generally must purchase their food, and as such require a regular cash income, which, in the cities of Bosnia-Herzegovina and other less developed countries, can be elusive.

Here again, the CGA offers a community-based response, promoting urban agriculture as a means of alleviating urbanization-related food insecurity. This response is by no means limited to Bosnia-Herzegovina. Indeed, food security experts increasingly view urban agriculture as 'an important supply source in developing-country urban food systems, a critical food–security valve for poor urban households'.[7] Widespread in Asia and Africa,

> (u)rban agriculture provides an estimated 15 per cent of all food consumed in urban areas and is likely to double that share in the next couple of decades. Cities with more advanced urban agriculture sectors, particularly in Asia, have become largely self-sufficient in higher-valued, nutritious perishables. Some cities even export surpluses abroad.[8]

Urban agriculture is common in Bosnia-Herzegovina, but limited access to land and the expense of inputs mean that relatively few actually avail themselves of the benefits. The CGA, by providing the land and inputs, removes these obstacles to participation. Moreover, the association's project directors are on hand to offer suggestions so that participants can maximize their yields. Participants thus gain valuable knowledge which they may pass on to other urbanites interested in growing food. Project staff are also keenly aware of the hazards of inappropriate urban agriculture (effluent run-off, contaminated soil, etcetera) and are available as a resource to urban growers and local officials who may require advice on policy dealing with urban food production. As such, the CGA stands to play a crucial role in providing support and information on urban agriculture, which is likely to rise as urbanization, and the numbers of urban poor, increase throughout Bosnia-Herzegovina.

Ethnic Division

Distrust and recrimination remain strong across ethnic groups (chiefly Croat, Muslim, Roma and Serb) in Bosnia-Herzegovina. For many people, however, ethnic separation is less a personal choice than a political and demographic reality that lies beyond their control. Many – particularly in formerly diverse urban centres such as Sarajevo – cherish the memory of a pre-war Bosnia-Herzegovina where social lives, communities and even families were formed without regard to ethnicity or religion. Moreover, many are quick to distinguish between those relatively few persons who committed atrocities in the name of nationality during the war and the majority who wanted neither war nor separation from fellow citizens of different groups. The ethnically divided society that characterizes Bosnia-Herzegovina today took shape against the wishes of many if not most of the country's people.

It is within this group of tolerant citizens that crucial support will be found as returns pick up and some of Bosnia-Herzegovina's communities begin to regain a multi-ethnic composition. Yet there remains little opportunity for people among this group to interact across ethnicities. Neighbourhoods, schools, markets and workplaces remain effectively segregated. Renewal of relations among different groups will only begin if there are venues in which cross-group interaction may safely take place.

The CGA provides such a venue. Each garden has an ethnically mixed group of between 16 and 25 participant families, including Muslims, Croats, Roma and Serbs. In addition to the interaction made possible by working side by side on their plots, occasional social events give the participants a chance to get to know one another. In the case of the first garden, people of different ethnicities – who otherwise would have had no opportunity to interact with those outside their own group – made friends by virtue of spending an entire growing season together and sharing the experience of growing food for their families.

The provision of a space for positive cross-group interaction is valuable not only as a means of healing war-related wounds. As Bosnia-Herzegovina continues its economic and social transition, increased mobility and urbanization will, as noted above, bring increased diversity to the cities. This diversity has already gone beyond the country's three dominant groups. In Sarajevo, for example, a rapidly growing Chinese community has taken root in recent years. Despite Bosnia-Herzegovina's current economic doldrums, its proximity to Western Europe, educated population and post-Second World War industrial and infrastructural development mean that the country is poised to experience a fairly rapid rise in living standards when cleaner and more competent leaders come to power. In this event, the country is likely to face the same unprecedented immigration challenges currently facing recent European comers such as Ireland and Spain. Similarly, the systematic exclusion of the Roma people from the mainstream of Bosnia-Herzegovina life will be challenged by globalization-related mobility and legal reform. The CGA, by dedicating itself to inclusion and diversity, represents a positive community-based response to these challenges.

It is worth noting that the CGA staff reflect the project's commitment to diversity. Project staff include women and men from Bosnia's main ethnic groups. The establishment of an affirmative action policy for project staff will be a part of the overall development of the CGA in the coming years.

Environmental Strain and Degradation

Environmental concerns are easily overlooked in a crisis or post-crisis situation, where the imperatives of survival are paramount. Yet environmental factors in Bosnia-Herzegovina will have a significant impact on the country's future, and the more sustainable the approach taken to the country's economic development, the better for future generations. This is especially true in the context of increased foreign investment and trade, which will focus to a significant degree on exploitation of natural resources. Moreover, resource consumption and waste output, particularly in urban areas, will increase rapidly as the Bosnia-Herzegovina economy grows.

The CGA addresses environmental concerns in two significant ways. First, as noted above in the context of food security, urban food production is widely expected to play an important role in creating sustainable cities in the coming century. Producing food close to consumers cuts down on transportation, reducing food costs, waste and fossil fuel use.[9] Other potential benefits include:

> improved hydrological functioning through soil and water conservation, micro-climate improvements, avoided costs of disposal of the recycled urban wastes (wastewater and solid waste), improved biodiversity, and greater recreational and aesthetic values of green space.[10]

There are environmental risks to urban food production as well, including run-off of fertilizers and other inputs into drinking water sources, microbial contamination of soil and water, and air pollution from organic matter and nitrates.[11] Recognizing these risks, the CGA will address the environmental dangers of urban food production itself. CGA staff are committed to using environ-

Living in Hope

mentally friendly methods in the gardens, and are devoting a portion of one of the gardens to the production of organic food. In this sense the CGA, as it grows in the coming years, will stand as a model for green farming techniques for the rest of the country, especially as contacts are developed with the government and other community gardening organizations around the world.

Governance

Bosnia-Herzegovina's continued integration into the world economy brings potential opportunities and difficulties. Among the former are: economic growth, poverty alleviation, job creation and equality of all citizens before the law. Among the latter are: increased socio-economic inequalities, environmental degradation and the vulnerability of particular groups to inflation and job market shifts. The mix of these potential positives and negatives is yet to be seen. Globalization is inevitable, but not inevitably positive or negative. That outcome depends on how the process is managed, which in turn depends on the quality of local and national governance.

In contemporary Bosnia-Herzegovina, that quality is universally considered to be exceedingly poor. Dedicated above all to retaining power, dominant political figures engage in obstructionist tactics to prevent legal reforms and have refused to relinquish state control over utilities and other enterprises, which provide a ready source of cash for political and personal purposes. Allegations of corruption have reached the highest level of government. According to a recent poll, the people of Bosnia-Herzegovina consider corruption to be the second most pressing issue facing the country, after the economy. In another poll, 68 per cent of respondents 'said they think all or nearly all Bosnia and Herzegovina politicians are corrupt', a majority adding that they had been 'directly affected by corruption'.

International actors can bring some pressure to bear in the fight against corruption, but serious progress depends on increased public accountability and a strong civil society. Herein lies the CGA's most challenging but potentially most important role. Beyond providing opportunities for food production and cross-ethnic interaction to participants, the CGA can have a broader impact by establishing links with similarly oriented groups around the world, as well as with policy makers and the media. By monitoring and calling public attention to issues of urban food insecurity, vulnerable groups and environmental concerns, the CGA will influence public policy in these areas and contribute to Bosnia-Herzegovina's nascent but burgeoning civil society.

For most people in Bosnia-Herzegovina, meeting basic needs is a daily struggle. The war and the removal of a safety net upon which generations had come to rely have forced many to develop new survival strategies. Among the most common of these is emigration. In a recent poll 62 per cent of the young people surveyed said they would leave the country if they had the chance. Some 10,000 a year do in fact emigrate. Black market economic activity is also common, due to the onerous tax and regulation burdens imposed on entrepreneurs by the government, and to illicit connections between influential business people and politicians. Other, more destructive responses to the changes, including organized crime, drug abuse and suicide, are also apparent.

The CGA is one of a growing number of community organizations dedicated to finding new, positive community responses to these difficult challenges. CGA staff aspire to building a national network of community gardens, addressing hunger and unemployment at the individual level as well as the broader issues outlined above. In order to accomplish this goal, the CGA is developing a management structure capable of sustaining a complex and geographically dispersed organization. Currently, management of the CGA involves joint participation by local and AFSC international staff. The high failure rate of Bosnian NGOs attempting to make the transition from international surrogate to viable local organization underscores how difficult this shift can be. For the CGA, the transition to full local control will involve the development of professional advisory, executive, outreach, fundraising, accounting, personnel and self-assessment mechanisms. It is anticipated that the Community Garden Association of Bosnia-Herzegovina will be a fully independent local organization by 2004, and that it will contribute significantly to community-based development and social change in the country for many years thereafter.

Notes

1 United Nations Development Programme, Independent Bureau for Humanitarian Issues, *Human Development Report, Bosnia and Herzegovina 2000 (Youth)*, p. 35.

2 International Crisis Group, *Bosnia's Refugee Logjam Breaks: Is the International Community Ready?* (Brussels: International Crisis Group, 31 May 2000), p. 4.

3 Recent pension law reforms imposed on Bosnia-Herzegovina by the Office of the High Representative were met by widespread opposition among beneficiaries. While the reforms were necessary given the corruption, inequality, inefficiency and insolvency that characterized the previous system, the requirement that pension payments be timely and tied to available resources is likely to result in diminished pensions for some seniors in the short to medium term. See Office of the High Representative, *Economic Reform and Reconstruction in Bosnia and Herzegovina Newsletter* (Sarajevo), Vol. 4, No. 1 (January 2001).

4 These include Serbs and Croats in Muslim-dominated Bosnia, Muslims and Croats in Republika Srpska, Muslims and Serbs in Croat-dominated Herzegovina, and Roma communities throughout the country. See Organization for Security and Cooperation in Europe (OSCE) Mission to Bosnia and Herzegovina, *Mission Reports on Human Dimension Activities*, report to Human Dimension Implementation Meeting, Warsaw, 17–27 October 2000 (OSCE, 2000).

5 'In the municipal elections in April 2000, women in B & H made history

with 18 per cent women elected, three times as many women as had been elected in the last municipal elections, and higher than any local election result ever in B & H.' *Ibid.*, p. 16.

6 'The World Bank ... estimated that the 1990s would see an increase from 400 million to one billion urban people living in absolute poverty; UNDP estimated a 76 per cent increase in urban poor during the 1990s and a decrease in rural poor during the same period.' FAO Committee on Agriculture, discussion paper, 'Urban and Peri-Urban Agriculture', Food and Agriculture Organization, 1999, http://www.fao.org/unfao/bodies/COAG/COAG15/x0076e.htm

7 Luc J. A. Mougeot, 'The Hidden Significance of Urban Agriculture', in International Food Policy Research Institute, 'Achieving Urban Food and Nutrition Security in the Developing World', *2020 Focus 3*, Brief 1 of 10, August 2000, http://www.ifpri.org/2020/focus/focus03.htm

8 *Ibid.*

9 Transportation costs can add as much as 90 per cent to urban food costs, while losses during transport of perishable foods can reach as high as 35 per cent. Olivio Argenti, 'Feeding the Cities: Food Supply and Distribution', in International Food Policy Research Institute, 'Achieving Urban Food and Nutrition Security'.

10 FAO Committee on Agriculture, 'Urban and Peri-Urban Agriculture', p. 7.

11 *Ibid.*

A Fair Deal?

John Feffer & Karin Lee

The Japanese economic miracle, which lifted a war-devastated country to the pinnacle of the world economy in less than two generations, was built with the help of the people and resources of all of Asia. Japanese companies have set up a manufacturing assembly line throughout the region to take advantage of low wages and cheap raw materials. Japanese consumers eat Thai shrimp, dine off wooden tables made from rare tropical trees from Malaysia, dress in clothes produced in China, and rely on electronics components manufactured in the Philippines. As with other industrialized countries, Japan's wealth depends a great deal on the hard work of people in the developing world. This dependency on the rest of Asia – and the negative impact of Japanese consumerism – is not well known within Japan.

Journalist Yayori Matsui has devoted much of her life to revealing Japan's true relationship with the region. She has published numerous articles and books about Japan's colonial role in the Second World War, particularly in the drafting of women into sexual slavery, and she has also chronicled Japan's economic exploitation in the post-war era. Yayori Matsui frequently meets with people at the Asia-Pacific Women's Centre, which she helped found. In the meeting room are boxes of materials – research, journals, shadow reports – on women's activities around the world. The Centre acts as a clearinghouse for women in this region. But Yayori Matsui is a clearinghouse unto herself. She loves to tell stories about people who, like herself, have come up with innovative projects that reveal Japan to the Japanese.

Take the case of the professor at Sofia University. 'He set up a project for his students to trace the cycle of different commodities such as shrimp and coconut oil,' Yayori Matsui explains.

One group of students traced the product history of pet food for cats. They went to the Philippines and Malaysia to see how the tuna is caught in very poor boats, how cheaply the fish is sold, how poor the fishermen's lives are. Then the students went to Indonesia where the fish is brought into modern ports built in part with Japan Overseas Development Assistance money. There they witnessed how the price of fish eaten by local people goes up because of the emphasis on exports. From there they went to Thailand to visit the pet food factory and witness the terrible working conditions. They watched as Japanese labels are put on the cans for export only. Finally they went to the supermarkets in Japan to see the pet food sold. From this experience they wrote a booklet, *The Cat that Ate Asia*. This project really forced the students to think about how much better cats in Japan are treated than people in Thailand.

Not far from the Women's Centre, in the Tokyo neighbourhood of Jiyugoaka, is the office of Global Village, an organization founded ten years ago by Safia Minney, an Englishwoman of Swiss and Indian parentage. Global Village has built relations with 70 producer groups throughout Asia, Africa and Latin America and has managed to improve the lives of thousands of farmers and handicrafts makers. Through a network of shops around Japan, Global Village sells fair trade products such as chocolate, organically grown cotton shirts, naturally dyed hemp twine, carvings from Kenya, dried mangoes and colourful postcards made in Zimbabwe.

Safia Minney's office is what a true world trade organization headquarters should look like. Samples of natural products fill the space. On a corkboard hang pictures of amateur models from Africa and Asia, spices in plastic bags, an organic coffee bag, swathes of natural fabric, display tags. There is a T-shirt large enough for three people and the text of the major codes of conduct developed for the clothing industry. It will be displayed as a visual prop in a long-term campaign to demonstrate the impact of corporations on people around the world. Global Village does not shrink from taking on an advocacy role – spreading information about fair working conditions, environmentalism and Japan's impact on the world to consumers and activists throughout the country.

'There are several fair trade organizations in Japan,' Safia Minney says.

> But we're the only one that is doing advocacy work. We're not uncomfortable doing political work because we're self-financed. We do WTO work, we were on the streets in Seattle, we launched a world fair trade day three years ago here in Japan. We believe that the political has to go hand-in-hand with creating good examples of fair trading practice.

The good examples of trading practice have been good for business. Global Village is growing rapidly, by 40 to 50 per cent each year. 'As an NGO and an ethical business, we can demonstrate that fair trade works, that we can make money,' Safia Minney explains.

Yayori Matsui and Safia Minney have many stories to tell about fair trade and what it represents in the globalization debate. They are both born communicators and feel strongly about the need to go beyond rhetoric and work directly with people on economic development. Interviewed separately, they echoed each other at many points, as though they were talking to one another through the medium of the interviewers. The journalist and the business-woman, although approaching the subject from slightly different angles, both believe that economic alternatives must lead to concrete economic gains and political empowerment for producers and consumers.

Organizing Alternatives

The fair trade movement formally began at the end of the 1960s. Non-profit organizations and world shops began to spring up around Europe and the US to promote trade that benefited the disadvantaged producers in poorer countries around the world. The first products included tea and coffee, cocoa and bananas, although the Mennonites were concentrating on handicrafts in their Ten Thousand Villages project.[1] The Body Shop, which started in 1976 in Brighton, England, perhaps brought the issue of 'fair trade' more publicity worldwide than any other concern. Although dedicated to non-animal-tested products and more advantageous deals for growers and extractors in the Third World, the Body Shop has not been without its detractors, who claim that the billion-dollar enterprise is more rhetoric than reality.[2]

In Japan, the fair trade movement started in the mid-1980s, with an emphasis on food products. Alternative Trade Japan, for instance, focused almost exclusively on arranging fair trade deals on prawns. The Japan Committee for Negros Campaign pioneered fair trade in bananas with Philippine growers. In the 1990s, Japanese organizations began to spread into the handicraft realm. In 1991, Safia Minney began Global Village.

Safia Minney grew up near the original Body Shop and later worked for the company for six months when it launched its first shop in Japan. There is, however, a big difference between the Body Shop and Global Village. While the Body Shop dabbles in fair trade (using some natural extracts in shampoos), Global Village sells nothing but fair trade goods.

The range of Global Village's relationships is impressive. For instance, it buys organic cotton from the Vidarhba Organic Farmers Association (VOFA) in the Indian state of Maharastra. VOFA has revived traditional Indian agricultural techniques that were virtually destroyed by the Green Revolution's emphasis on chemical fertilizers and pesticides. It uses natural pest management such as sprays made of garlic and chilli. And instead of chemical fertilizers, it plants nitrogen–fixing crops such as lentils in between the cotton rows. Global Village finances the organic cotton certification and buys over 60 per cent of VOFA's harvest.

In Kenya, Global Village buys handicrafts from Bombolulu Workshops, where the majority of the 160 artisans have physical disabilities. The artisans design jewellery, make clothes and fashion wooden carvings. Bombolulu is run like a business, with marketing and design departments. It holds fashion shows. It is dependent for 95 per cent of its overseas sales on fair trade organizations such as Global Village. In a country with 25 per cent unemployment, Bombolulu is providing well–paid work for artisans whose physical disabilities and lack of formal education might otherwise keep them entirely out of the workforce.

Sometimes Global Village has played an important role in building up enterprises through product development and appropriate technology. Take, for example, the case of the Bagda Enterprise, which makes hemp twine. The Bagda Enterprise is located in Agailhjara, a river estuary in Bangladesh. To get there, Safia Minney had to take a truck from Dacca and then a series of boats. She went for the first time four years ago, when she was six months pregnant. When she finally arrived in Agailhjara she found a group of women making hemp twine by hand.

'There was no engine,' she says. 'So they made an engine with their hands to twist the hemp and give it strength. The programme had fallen on hard times at that time and they'd had to retire people. They had this one type of hemp twine and that was all. They didn't know what other kinds of products to sell.'

Borrowing from experiences in other parts of the world, Safia Minney immediately leapt into action. 'We did a workshop to show them how to use natural dyes. We organized a crochet workshop to use natural dyes and knitting and twine to make bags. We linked up with a fair trade group making handmade paper products nearby in order to make other products possible.'

When she returned to Agailhjara in December 2000, Safia Minney found a very different scene.

> The 25-strong group had grown into more than 80 women. They'd started to bring in workers from nearby villages to help with production. They'd gotten a huge order from the Body Shop. The product quality level had improved. They'd managed to move the centralized workshop back to the people's homes. So they were making the paper at home, crushing the water hyacinth, sunning it on a steel pan in the sunshine. Many people who had lost their houses three years ago in floods had rebuilt their houses. In that area of Bangladesh you rarely see two-storey houses and one of the women had built a two-storey house.

Trade as Solidarity

When she was a journalist at *Asahi Shimbun*, one of Japan's largest newspapers, Yayori Matsui uncovered many of the early stories of communities in Asia that organized alternative marketing and fair trade organizations.

'In the case of Weaving for Alternatives in Thailand,' Yayori Matsui says,

> many women are using traditional skills for local empowerment. These skills used to be looked down on. But nowadays they can use these skills to be better off economically – and they are making beautiful artistic creations. Twenty-four villages are members of the Pan Mai cooperative – Pan Mai in Thai means 'many different kinds of seeds or plants' – and in each village there is a women's committee for weaving. Each committee sends a representative to learn bookkeeping and management as well as training in dying, weaving and spinning. They don't buy the materials, but instead grow everything. The colour is only taken from the plants or tree bark or fruits or wild flowers – these are very beautiful natural colours.

The weaving cooperative is not merely a workplace. 'They

have also started other projects,' Yayori Matsui continues, 'for instance, building a gas tank for the community for income. They started an insurance scheme for funerals – because poor people can't afford funerals. Members contribute small sums and when one dies, they withdraw money for the funeral.'

Some of the first attempts at alternative trade faced significant obstacles. On the Philippine island of Negros, for instance, farmer cooperatives created a banana project that traded directly with consumer cooperatives in Japan. Negros is the fourth largest island of the Philippines. It is resource-rich, but the people of Negros remain quite poor. After the fall of the Marcos regime, development money flowed into Negros, but the aid couldn't be absorbed and many new enterprises failed. The Japan Committee for Negros Campaign joined with the Negros Relief Rehabilitation Center to emphasize 'trade not aid'. They set up an organic banana project to bypass the corporate banana growers that had such a negative impact on the Philippine workers and the Philippine land. Because of the chemicals used in the growing process, commercial bananas may have a negative effect on Japanese consumers as well. The first shipments from Negros arrived in 1989 – the Balangon variety that Japanese favour and Filipinos consider not sweet enough – and were sold throughout the well-organized consumer cooperative system in Japan.[3]

'The people in Negros were very politically organized,' Yayori Matsui recalls.

When the sugar cane industry was affected by the fall in sugar prices, many people in Negros lost their jobs. The people tried to solve this problem by themselves, not to get aid from outside. When the Negros campaign started in Japan, we wanted to start a very equal partnership between people in Japan and people in Negros, not a one-sided relationship of donor and recipient, not 'us' giving 'them' charity. So we established an equal partnership, and many people in Japan learned from the people of Negros.

The Negros experiment was also important because of the influence it had on other groups in the region. According to Yayori Matsui,

> One Hong Kong group learned a lot from the Negros project and started a lily bulb project with two villages in mainland China. This group wanted to choose a different consumer item, not bananas but lily bulbs, based on the local situation. I think the lily bulb project is still successful, because consumer groups in Hong Kong are still selling the lily bulbs. It's a very good consumer group and it also promotes solidarity with people in mainland China. In both cases, the people were empowered because they did it by themselves – they learned agricultural skills and management skills.

Who Benefits?

One striking aspect of the producer groups that work with Global Village – which vary in size from a couple of dozen artisans to nearly 20,000 – is the disproportionate number of women workers. Concern Bangladesh, which produces incense and knit lace jewellery, is run by 1,800 women and no men. Saffy Handicrafts in the Philippines, which makes bags and accessories, employs 700 women and 350 men. The ThaiCraft Association, which makes silver accessories and silk scarves, employs 7,500 women and 500 men.

Through the experience of working in a fair trade company, many women not only are able to support their families and earn incomes equivalent to men, but also learn new skills and gain new confidence. Many women move into leadership positions in the enterprises. Yayori Matsui noticed that among the economic projects run by women there was an interesting effect beyond the workplace.

> Once they form these groups, domestic violence decreases. In the

two villages in China involved in the lily bulb project, the members of the women's credit union talk to each other all the time. If one member's husband beats his wife, it is known by the other members. The husband becomes ashamed, so it's a form of control. The same thing happened in Thailand after the weaving groups started. At the beginning, the husbands were not happy. In these villages, women are not supposed to even leave the village. But later, the husbands realized that women can earn some money. So eventually the husbands began to help these weaving projects by repairing the weaving tools. Because women are empowered, they talk to each other. In that sense, the relationship between men and women has improved.

Many of the producer groups working with Global Village target certain populations or have specific missions central to their trading activity. Bombolulu in Kenya, for instance, employs artisans with physical disabilities, particularly those who are victims of polio. Tara Projects in India works with families in an effort to ensure that children do not become labourers. Tara has set up schools and vocational training centres for the children of poor families. Indeed, it is a rare producer group that doesn't sponsor additional programmes: on health and nutrition, literacy, technical training and savings. The Cocla organic coffee enterprise in Peru or the Bhaktapur Craft Printers in Nepal are not simply workplaces: they address the many needs and interests of their employees, the families of employees, and the communities in which the employees live.

Another key concern of Global Village is the environment. Safia Minney lobbied to insert eco-friendly production criteria into the Code of Practice of the International Federation for Alternative Trade, a document that guides fair trade organizations around the world. Global Village itself follows five environmental policies: non-destruction of the forests, non-pollution of the atmosphere, non-pollution of the water, protection of people and livelihoods and avoidance of waste. These policies translate into the use of recyclable materials, the promotion of organic farming, and a programme to encourage the use of wood from fast-growing trees such as mango and jacaranda for carvings.

Obstacles

One of the challenges for the fair trade movement is to ensure that the products continue to qualify for the label. 'Before we start working with a producer group,' Safia Minney explains,

> we give them a detailed questionnaire on each product area. Different products are produced in different working conditions. Some producers work at home, others at small factories. We try to compare the wages at the producer group to those of other workers in the area. But sometimes we're talking about areas with 50 to 60 per cent unemployment.

After the relationship is established, Safia Minney and her colleagues personally visit the projects. In the case of India and Bangladesh, she visits the projects twice a year. She and her colleagues crunch a lot of numbers in order to determine fair wages and fair prices. But they are also dealing with a number of difficult-to-price items, such as access to a literacy programme or the availability of loans at advantageous rates. The most effective monitoring technique is to look at the lives of the workers.

'If they've worked for two years for fair trade, you expect to see improvement in the workers' lives,' she says. 'You can see how much they are saving, if their children can go to school, if their homes have improved. Maybe they rebuilt their house or put a proper roof on it. Maybe they built a small shop where their husband can work.'

Many of the producer groups working with Global Village show remarkable success in short periods of time. But there are no certainties in the world of fair trade. If the orders dry up, then workers are laid off. 'There is no guarantee just because it's fair trade, the orders will continue,' Safia Minney says regretfully. She cites the example of one handicraft producer that didn't make enough investment into product development and marketing and couldn't survive. Then there are the conventional traders who make similar products and market them head-to-head against fair-trade products, but at lower prices. For Bombolulu, the combination of torrential rains in 1998 that ruined buildings and an upsurge in ethnic violence in Kenya that cut into tourism revenues sent the company into the red. In 2000, however, with the help of its buyers Bombolulu was able to break even.

Global Village has only pulled out of one project – in Madras, India. 'Clearly the manager was not running it very well. He wasn't very competent. He was using the younger women in ways that weren't very professional. You didn't feel a sense of trust in the way it was being run.' But in all the other 70 relationships, she hastens to add, 'there haven't been any scandals. We work very close with our producers.'

Yayori Matsui explains that the Negros banana project has encountered some difficulties in recent years. The project prospered in part because the organizers were very politically conscious. But the heightened political sensibilities also led to factionalism and conflict. She explains:

> People who are fighting against a global force suffer from political splits, because the power they are fighting is too strong – the banana empire is so strong, the global market is so strong. But it did have some success, why? Because it was people-to-people trade. People who grow bananas and people who eat bananas have a direct trade. There is no big company that profits from the banana trade. This project was useful for both sides.

Consumer Society

Japan is a strong consumer society. Although credit card debt is low and the rate of savings is high, Japanese citizens are encouraged by advertising, the government and a gift-giving culture to buy as much as they can to boost the economy. There are not many counter-messages that rein in the spending.

As Yayori Matsui explains, however, there is one very strong movement that challenges mindless consumerism.

> The Seikatsu Cooperative club – *seikatsu* means 'life' in Japanese – started in the 1960s when a group of housewives began to buy milk collectively. The Seikatsu cooperative has been quite different from the traditional consumers' movement, which has been concerned with price or the safety of food. This group wants to start an alternative lifestyle based on less consumerism, less energy consumption. The scale of the cooperative is quite large – 250,000 members. They are trying to establish links with producers, farmers who grow organic foods. This group won the Alternative Livelihood award – the alternative Nobel – so it is internationally recognized. And it has been very helpful in empowering women members.

The Seikatsu Cooperative has not restricted its activities to buying products. It has also established a workers' collective. 'Many wives want to earn money but prefer not to be employed by big companies,' Yayori Matsui says. 'They don't want to work in such a competitive society, so they prefer to start their own small businesses in the field of food supply or food processing.' Finally, the Seikatsu Cooperative has become large enough to flex its political muscles, electing a couple of hundred women to local office all over the country. 'At the same time,' Yayori Matsui says, 'there are many criticisms of the Seikatsu Cooperative. The top leaders are men, but the ordinary members are women.'

Have there been any other challenges to consumerism that have had any effect? Yayori Matsui cites a recent book by the

Thai environmentalist Sinith Sittirak, *The Daughters of Development*.

Before going to Canada to study environmental studies, she looked down on her mother's lifestyle as very old-fashioned. Her mother used shells instead of plastic bags. She relied on her garden for everything. Sinith Sittirak felt very ashamed. But after she studied environmentalism she realized the importance of preserving the ecological lifestyle of her mother. So she wrote about this, using her mother's lifestyle for environmental education in Thailand today.

'At the same time,' Yayori Matsui admits,

when I look at her mother's ecological life, of course it's nice, but realistically how many people can adopt this kind of lifestyle in the urbanized '90s? How can the inhabitants of what Saskia Sassen calls 'global cities' such as Tokyo or New York live according to this traditional lifestyle? I have reservations about the possibility of expanding this kind of lifestyle or influencing structural change this way. Of course I quite support her very strong criticism of consumerism, how it destroys people's relationships, makes people very competitive, very egoistic. At the same time we must find alternatives that can be practised more widely and can be influential in changing the mainstream economic system. There are many attempts, but they are experiments only.

We ask her for more examples of these 'experiments'. She thinks about this question for a moment before answering.

In Thailand, too, I think that Buddhism has had an impact, because Buddhism has a philosophy of simple life. Even Thai feminists are very interested in Buddhism. They think it is a more ecological religion than Christianity, because Christianity has been more destructive of nature. According to Buddhism, people should live together with nature. Have you read the book written by a Thai woman journalist, Sanitsuda Kochai, *Behind the Smile: Voices of Thailand*? It is a very good book. She went to many rural areas and talked to many people victimized by development. She admires those who have tried to lead a simple, ecological life. She talked to many 'development monks' who have tried to develop their villages by 'integrated farming'. The monks teach how to make a fish pond, plant fruit trees and vegetables, and raise pigs. This integrated farming is spreading. In India, too, there are so many alternative groups, many of them influenced by Gandhi's philosophy, that want to live a more simple life, consuming less energy, and recycling more.

Challenging Japan

As Yayori Matsui points out, economic alternatives will have a global impact only if they influence the mainstream system. And that means changing the behaviour of people in the industrialized countries of the world: the United States, Europe and Japan. These countries consume the lion's share of the world's resources.

Safia Minney started Global Village with this goal in mind: to change the consumption patterns of the Japanese. She aimed to provide consumers with enough information to support environmental initiatives, buy environmentally sound products, and demand more environmentally sound policies from local authorities. 'There were a lot of citizen groups on a local level,' she says. 'But there was no support from the side of the local authorities.' Today, Japanese citizens are more environmentally aware.

At the same time, environmental and fair trade considerations are still not driving consumer demand. 'We probably sell the most attractive products in the world,' she says. 'We have the nicest produced catalogue of fair trade products. Why? Because we're in Japan. No one buys stuff in Japan because of fair trade or because of ecology. They buy it because it's well-designed.'

Yayori Matsui has expended a great deal of energy trying to show to Japanese consumers the true cost of their consumption. Shrimp consumption in Japan, for instance, is staggering.

Our centre sent a study tour to Malaysia where we visited the Penang consumers' movement, which has launched a campaign on shrimp. Many coastal areas in Pakistan, Thailand, Bangladesh and elsewhere have been converted to shrimp – there has been big ecological destruction, farmers have lost their lands, and many people have been killed for resisting shrimp cultivation. The first thing is that we must share this information about the situation of shrimp cultivation with Japanese.

What then? Some Japanese activists have proposed a boycott of shrimp. 'But a boycott campaign is very difficult,' Yayori Matsui says. 'Many boycotts have been proposed. Most of these boycotts have failed. I'm a little bit sceptical about a shrimp boycott. It's so difficult for ordinary people to consume less.'

In some cases, the Japanese government has been actively involved in the despoliation of the environment in the region. Take the case of tropical timbers. 'Japan is the largest importer of tropical timbers,' Yayori Matsui explains.

Half of the timber we import comes from Sarawak, one state in Malaysia. Sarawak is a country of indigenous people. I went to Sarawak and wrote about the plight of the indigenous people there – their protests, the blockading of logging roads. The situation is so painful because many people have to work in the logging industry in order to make money. And they get killed. I wrote about the situation for the people here in Japan. Here they've formed the Japan Forest Action Network and they've been campaigning very strongly in many ways. They've been successful in a sense. The import of timber has decreased. But again we have to link up with other countries. After Japan reduced import of tropical timbers, Korea and Taiwan increased their imports! We had a workshop in Korea to appeal to the Korean public about this – we have to have at least regional cooperation on this issue.

Challenging the Japanese government has meant challenging the Overseas Development Agency (ODA), which disburses aid to countries around the world. ODA money has poured into building the infrastructure necessary to farm shrimp or extract tropical timber. 'In the 1980s, there were so many campaigns against Japanese official development assistance and I was one of the very strong critics,' Yayori Matsui says.

> Gradually there has been some kind of change. In the beginning, the ODA didn't want to work at all with NGOs. But now they have agreed to work together with grassroots NGOs. Or they have adopted a little more transparency. For instance, on the Sarawak issue, the government did not want to release the data about economic aid that had been used for logging. Nowadays there is more transparency because of pressure, so you can get information about these development projects. Basically, of course, the policy is for the benefit not of the people in the receiving company but of the companies or the state. It's the same in other donor countries. But here in Japan at least there is growing participation by NGOs – that is some improvement.

A Systemic Alternative?

Does the fair trade movement offer a full-scale alternative to the global marketplace of unrestrained competition, environmental degradation and low wages? Perhaps this is not a fair question at this point. The movement is still in its infancy. Producers and consumers are just beginning to connect with one another.

'When we organized the Asian Women's Alternatives in Action in Beijing, we talked about how to link up with other groups, how to expand these dots and make them into a line,' Yayori Matsui says.

> But we're not yet so successful as to affect the mainstream economic system in each country. Also, without the strong will or enthusiasm of the people involved, these projects don't continue. Most people just want to make more money in the ordinary market. So it's not so easy

for people to be idealistic or politically concerned. Those who can do this kind of project should have a certain different kind of human nature; they have to have some kind of vision of the future, or they must see the meaning of life differently. For many people, making money is not so important. At the same time, global economic forces are so strong – small-scale grassroots projects encounter so much difficulty. To change the whole structure? I'm rather pessimistic.

Safia Minney, on the other hand, remains optimistic, in part perhaps because her business is expanding and they've just opened a new branch in England.

We are setting a good example of business practice that will empower small-scale producers and farmers. We are reaching out as widely as possible to members of the public to politicize them, with the product as a tool. People will buy a product in the shop on its design merits and then realize that there is a whole world out there and they have to think about these things ethically.

Notes

1 For more information on the origins of the fair trade movement, see Martin Kunz, *Fair Trade* (Wiesbaden, Germany: World University Service, 1999). The Ten Thousand Villages project began in 1946 and became an official Mennonite Central Committee programme in the 1970s.

2 See, e.g., Jon Entine, 'Rain-forest Chic', Globe and Mail Report on Business Magazine, October 1995.

3 The story of the Negros project can be found in Raymundo Tenefrancia, 'Grassroots Trading Initiatives in Negros and the Philippines', *Asian Exchange*, vol. 15, no. 1 & 2, 1999, pp. 85–110.

Resources

General

Books

Sarah Anderson and John Cavanaugh with Thea Lee, *Field Guide to the Global Economy*. New York: The New Press, 2000.

Richard Barnett and John Cavanaugh, *Global Dreams: Imperial Corporations and the New World Order*. New York: Touchstone Press of Simon and Schuster, 1994.

Jeremy Brecher and Tim Costello, *Global Village or Global Pillage: Economic Reconstruction from the Bottom Up*. Boston: South End Press, 1998.

Jeremy Brecher, Tim Costello and Brendan Smith, *Globalization from Below: the Power of Solidarity*. Boston: South End Press, 2000.

Miriam Ching Louie and Linda Burnham, *WEdGE – Women's Education in the Global Economy*. Women of Color Resource Center, 2000. 2288 Fulton Street, Suite 103, Berkeley, CA 94704-1449. *(A workbook of activities, games, skits, and strategies.)*

Herman E. Daly and John B. Cobby, Jr, *For the Common Good*. Boston: Beacon Press, 1989.

Kevin Danaher, (ed.), *Democratizing the Global Economy. The Battle against the World Bank and the IMF*. Available from the 50 Years is Enough Network for $20. Call 202-IMF-BANK.

Charles Derber, *Corporation Nation: How Corporations Are Taking over Our Lives and What We Can Do about It*. New York: St Martin's Press, 1998.

Susan George, *A Fate Worse than Debt*. New York: Grove, 1990.

Susan George, *The Debt Boomerang*. London: Pluto: 1991.

Susan George, *The Lugano Report*. London: Pluto, 1999.

William Greider, *One World, Ready or Not: the Manic Logic of Global Capitalism*. New York: Simon and Schuster, 1997. *(Long but very clear introduction to global production and investment.)*

Martha Honey, *Ecotourism and Sustainable Development: Who Owns Paradise?* Washington, DC: Island Press, 1999.

Susan Joekes, *Women and the New Trade Agenda*, New York: UNIFEM, 1995.

David C. Korten, *When Corporations Rule the World*. Kumarian Press, 1995. *(How corporate power rose, its intellectual basis, how the system works, what it does to people, and one man's vision of an alternative.)*

Paul Krugman, *The Accidental Theorist*. New York: Norton, 1999.

Arthur MacEwan, *Neo-Liberalism or Democracy? Economic Strategy, Markets, and Alternatives for the Twenty-first Century*. New York: St Martin's Press, 1999.

Peter Madden, *A Raw Deal: Trade and the World's Poor*. London: Christian Aid, 1992. *(Examines the relationship between trade policy and practice and economic deprivation.)*

John Madeley, *Hungry for Trade*. London: Zed Books, 2000. *(Overview of how international trade and changes in agricultural practice due to globalization affect developing countries.)*

John Madeley, *Trade and the Poor*. London: Intermediate Technology Publications, 1992, 1996. *(A critical look at international trade arrangements and organizations and the vulnerability of the poor in developing countries.)*

Majid Rahnema, and Victoria Bawtree (eds.). *The Post-Development Reader*. London: Zed Books, 1997. *(Excellent essays on women, neocolonialism, the environment, development and official ideologies.)*

Andrew Ross, (ed.), *No Sweat: Fashion, Free Trade, and the Rights of Garment Workers*. London: Verso, 1997. *(Cutting-edge design, and analysis of the global garment assembly line.)*

Vandana Shiva, *Stolen Harvest: the Hijacking of the Global Food Supply*. Boston: South End Press, 2000.

UNDP, *Human Development Report, 1999*. New York: Oxford University Press, 1999.

UNDP, *Human Development Report, 2000*. New York: Oxford University Press, 2000.

Videos on Globalization and Free Trade

Banking on Life and Debt, 30 minutes. Narrated by Martin Sheen. Produced by Maryknoll World Productions, PO Box 308, Maryknoll, NY, 10545-0308, 800-227-8523. *(The World Bank, the IMF, structural adjustment, and three case studies: Brazil, Phillipines, Ghana.)*

Deadly Embrace, 30 minutes. Elizabeth Canner, 617-666-5122 or <lizcanner@hotmail.com>. *(The World Bank, structural adjustment, and Nicaragua.)*

Global Village or Global Pillage, 28 minutes. Preamble Center's World Economy Project. *(How people around the world are fighting the 'race to the bottom'.)*

Life or Debt, 90 minutes. POV@pbs.org *(On debt and IMF policy in Jamaica.)*

WTO: In Whose Hands? 20 minutes. Women's Division General Board of Global Ministries, United Methodist Church, 1-800-305-9857.

Two Trevors Go to Washington. 27 minutes. Center for Economic Justice, 202/299-0020. *(The IMF/World Bank meetings and protests in April 2000 through the eyes of two South Africans.)*

Organizations and web sites

AFL-CIO: www.aflcio.org

American Friends Service Committee: www.afsc.org

Centre for Economic and Policy Research: www.cepr.net

Centre for Popular Economics (economic literacy): www.ctrpopec.org

Centre of Concern (analysis, public education, policy advocacy, theological reflection on global economic issues, human rights and gender): www.coc.org

Development GAP (trade, development, World Bank): www.developmentgap.org

Ecumenical Coalition for Economic Justice, Ontario, Canada: www.ece.acessv.com

50 Years Is Enough: www.50years.org

Friends of the Earth: www..foe.org

Institute for Agriculture and Trade Policy: www.iatp.org

Institute for Policy Studies (analysis, publications, media work): www.ips-dc.org

Jubilee/USA

    Contact: Maura Vanderslice, 222 E. Capitol St NE,

    Washington, DC 20003-1036.

    Phone: 202-783-3566. Fax: 202-546-4468.

    http://www.j2000usa.org

Oxfam International: www.oxfaminternational.org

Public Services International: psiamericas@igc.org

Quaker United Nations Office: www.quno.org

United for a Fair Economy: www.ufenet.org

United Nations Conference on Trade and Development (UNCTAD) (web site with links to the projects of UNCTAD and other agencies in the area of trade and development): www.unctad.org

United Nations Development Programme (UNDP) (humanitarian and development issues): www.undp.ba/home.html

United Nations High Commissioner for Refugees (UNHCR) (refugee and displaced person resettlement): www.unhcr.ba/

Women of Color Resource Center: www.coloredgirls.org

Women's International League for Peace and Freedom: (202) 546-6727

Publications

Alejandro Bendana, 'The Antiglobalization Movement: Obstacles and Opportunities', www.fpig.org/outside/commentary/2002/0201south.html.

Dollars and Sense: www.dollarsandsense.org

The Economist: www.economist.com

Global Exchange (news, analysis, activism concerning globalization and fair trade): www.globalexchange.org

Multi-National Monitor: www.essential.org/monitor

New Internationalist: www.newint.org

Peacework: www.afsc.org/peacewrk.htm

A Citizen's Guide to the World Trade Organization. Booklet (28 pp.) available from the Apex Press, Suite 3C, 777 UN Plaza, New York, NY 10017.

Economics Education: Building A Movement For Global Economic Justice. Available from the AFSC Praxis/Economic Justice Project, 6375 Dearborn, Chicago, IL60605.

False Profits: Who Wins, Who Loses When the IMF, World Bank, and WTO Come to Town. Available from 50 Years Is Enough Network: www.50years.org

Maquiladora Reader. Available from the AFSC, 1501 Cherry Street, Philadelphia.

The Insider: What I Learned at the World Economic Crisis, article by Joseph Stiglitz, New Republic Online, 4/7/2000.

Unpacking Globalization – a Popular Education Tool Kit. Publication of the Economic Literacy Action Network (ELAN) contains interactive workshops and support materials (145 pp.). Available from United for a Fair Economy, www.ufenet.org

Africa *(Chapter 5)*

Books

Makonnen Alemayehu, *Industrializing Africa: Development Options and Challenges for the Twenty-first Century.* Trenton, NJ: Africa World Press, 2000.

Michael Barrett Brown, *Africa's Choices after Thirty Years of the World Bank.* Boulder, CO: Westview Press, New York: Columbia University Press, 1997.

Thomas M. Callahy and John Ravenhill (eds.), *Hemmed in: Responses to Africa's Economic Decline.* New York: Columbia University Press, 1993.

Jerker Carlsson, Gloria Somolekae and Nicolas van de Walle, *Foreign Aid in Africa: Learning from Country Experiences.* Uppsala, Sweden: Nordiska Afrikainstitutet, 1997.

Corporate Council on Africa, *Doing Business with Africa, 2000/1,* Washington, DC: Corporate Council on Africa, 2000. 091667309X: available from Council on Foreign Relations Task Force, Promoting US Economic Relations with Africa. 1999.

Lual A. L. Deng, *Rethinking African Development: Toward a Framework for Social Integration and Ecological Harmony.* Trenton, NJ: Africa World Press, 1998.

Steve Kayizzi-Mugerwa, Adebayo Olukoshi and Lennart Wohlgemuth (eds.), *Towards a New Partnership with Africa.* Uppsala, Sweden: Nordiska Afrikainstitutet, 1998.

Carol Lancaster, *Aid to Africa: So Much to Do, So Little Done.* Chicago: University of Chicago Press, 1999.

Michael Maren, *The Road to Hell: the Ravaging Effects of Foreign Aid and International Charity.* New York: Free Press, 1997.

John Mihevc, *The Market Tells Them So: The World Bank and Economic Fundamentalism in Africa.* London: Zed Books, 1996.

Thandika Mkandawire and Charles C. Soludo, *Our Continent, Our Future: African Perspectives on Structural Adjustment.* Trenton, NJ and Asmara, Eritrea: Africa World Press, 1999.

Richard E. Mshomba, *Africa in the Global Economy.* Boulder, CO: Lynne Rienner Publishers, 2000.

Ann Paulson (ed.), *African Economies in Transition. Volume 1: Changing the Role of the State.* New York: Palgrave, 2000.

Ann Paulson (ed.), *African Economies in Transition. Volume 2: The Reform Experience.* New York: Palgrave, 1999.

Judith Randel et al. (eds), *The Reality of Aid.* Sterling, VA: Stylus, 2000.

Abdi Ismail Samatar, *An African Miracle*. 1999.

Margaret Snyder and Mary Tadesse, *African Women and Development: a History*. London: Zed Books, 1995.

Peter Veit (ed.), *Africa's Valuable Assets: a Reader in Natural Resource Management*. Washington: World Resources Institute, 1999.

World Bank, *Can Africa Claim the Twenty-first Century?* New York: Oxford University Press, 2000.

Organizations and web sites

Africa Action – New York Office

Contact: Aleah Bacquie, 50 Broad St, Suite 1701, New York, NY 10004.
Phone: 212-785-1024. Fax: 212-785-1078.
africafund@igc.org
http://www.theafricafund.org

Africa Action – Washington DC Office

Contact: Vicki Ferguson, Director of Education and Outreach,
110 Maryland Ave., NE, #508,
Washington, DC 20002.
Phone: 202-546-7961. Fax: 202-546-1545.
vlf@africapolicy.org
http://www.africapolicy.org

Africa Faith and Justice Network

Contact: Larry Goodwin or Carole Collins, Policy Analyst,
3035 Fourth St NE, Washington, DC 20017.
Phone: 202-832-3412. Fax: 202-832-9051.
afjn@afjn.org
http://www.afjn.org

Association of Concerned Africa Scholars

Contact: Jim Cason, Political Action Committee,
132 N. Carolina Ave., SE, Washington, DC 20003.
Phone: 202-547-5852. Fax: 202-546-7776.
jcason@mindspring.com
http://www.prairienet.org/acas

TransAfrica

Contact: Mwiza Munthali, Information Specialist,
1744 R St, NW, Washington, DC 20009.
Phone: 202/797-2301. Fax: 202/797-2382.
info@transforum.org
http://www.transafricaforum.org

Washington Office on Africa
    Contact: Leon P Spencer, Executive Director,
    212 East Capitol St, Washington, DC 20003.
    Phone: 202-547-7503. Fax: 202-547-7505.
    woa@igc.org
    http://www.woaafrica.org

For a list of web sites giving Africa Debt information see:
http://www.africapolicy.org/action/debt.htm

For a list of web sites on other economic issues see:
http://www.africapolicy.org/docs01/econ.shtml

Browsing the www.Africapolicy.org *web site will give a lot of key information.*

AMERICAS *(Chapters 3, 6 and 8)*

Books

Patricia Camacho and Vinicio Villalba, *Construcción de Sistemas de Comercialización Comunitaria.* Ecuador: MCCH/SID, 1997). *(A case study on the marketing of cacao in Ecuador by organized small-scale producers in the Maquita Cushunchic alternative trade network.)*

John Clark, *For Richer, for Poorer.* Oxford: OXFAM, 1986. *(An OXFAM report on Western connections with world hunger.)*

Comité Fronterizo de Obreras, *Six Years of NAFTA: a View from Inside the Maquiladoras.* Piedras Negras, Coahuila/Philadelphia, PA: CFO/AFSC Mexico–US Border Programme, October 1999.

Coordinador de la Sociedad Civil Centroamérica Solidaria, *Plataforma para la Transformación de Centroamerica en la Perspectiva del Desarrollo Human Sostenible.* Alforja: 2001. *(Platform for human development in Central America based on the positions of civil society organizations in Panama, San José, Costa Rica, Honduras, Nicaragua, El Salvador, Guatemala and Belize.)*

Fundación Arias para La Paz y el Progreso Humano, *Algunas Metodologías de Sostenibilidad: El Caso de la Red COMAL.* Costa Rica: 2001. *(A case study of the sustainability of the COMAL network in alternative marketing in Honduras.)*

Rachel Garst and Tom Barry, *Feeding the Crisis: US Food Aid and Farm Policy in Central America.* Lincoln and London: University of Nebraska Press, 1991. *(Analysis on food security, food aid and food as a political tool in Central America through the 1980s.)*

Duncan Green, *Silent Revolution: the Rise of Market Economics in Latin America.* Latin America Bureau, Ltd., Cassell, 1995. *(Analysis on economic and political trends in Latin America since 1973.)*

Cristobal Maldidier and Peter Marchetti, *El Campesino-Finquero y el Potencial Económico del Campesinado Nicaraguense.* Managua, Nicaragua: Nitlapán, 1996. *(An analysis of the economic, social and cultural potential of the the small and middle-scale rural enterprise in Nicaragua.)*

Hugo Noe Pino, 'The Structural Roots of Crisis: Economic Growth and Decline in Honduras 1950–1984'. PhD dissertation, University of Texas at Austin, 1988. *(An historical and economic analysis with ample statistical support which examines the agrarian, industrial and external sectors as well as trends and decline in growth in the Honduran economy.)*

Maria Jesús Pérez (ed.), *Mercado Ético con Calidad y Espiritualidad: Sistematización de la Experiencia de 15 Años de la Fundacion MCCH.* Quito: Imprefepp, 2000. *(History of the first 15 years of the Maquita Cushunchic Foundation and the construction of an alternative community-based marketing network in Ecuador.)*

Beat Schmid (ed.), *Libre Comercio: Promesas vs Realidad.* Mexico City, Mexico: Ediciones Boll, 2000. *(Collection of essays from El Salvador, Mexico, Brazil and other countries on globalization, its effects and its challenges in Latin America.)*

United Nations Development Programme, *Human Development Report, Honduras 1998.* Tegucigalpa: UNDP, 1998. *(Human development report with a special focus on inclusive development.)*

United Nations Development Programme, *Human Development Report, Honduras 1999.* Tegucigalpa: UNDP, 1999. *(Human development report with a special focus on the impact of Hurricane Mitch.)*

United Nations Development Programme, *State of the Region in Human Sustainable Development, Central America 1999, Report No. 1.* San José, Costa Rica: UNDP/EU, 1999. *(A report written from Central America with information and analysis components on the region as a whole and on special situations in each country.)*

Publications

Alternativas para el Desarrollo: A monthly publication in Spanish on economic and social development produced by the Fundación Nacional para el Desarrollo (FUNDE) in El Salvador. It includes frequent articles on international trade, its impact in Central America and alternative models. Subscriptions can be ordered via: FUNDE, Apdo. Postal 1774, Centro de Gobierno, San Salvador, El Salvador. funde@ejje.com

Alternatives for the Americas: Discussion Draft No. 3 prepared by the Hemispheric Social Alliance for the Second People's Summit of the Americas. Currently available at the following web site: http.//www.asc-hsa.org

Comercio y Desarrollo: Weekly bulletin edited by the Consejo de Investigacions para el Desarrollo de Centroamérica (CIDECA) in Guatemala. Written in Spanish and published via the Internet, the bulletin includes information on trade policy, globalization and alternative development models for Central America. For more information: cideca@intelnet.net.gt

El Fogón: A quarterly publication in Spanish of the COMAL network in Honduras, written principally for its affiliates. Subscriptions can be ordered via: COMAL,

Apdo. Postal 171, Siguatepeque, Comayagua, Honduras. comal@bigfoot.com

Revista Envío: Monthly magazine published in both English and Spanish by the University of Central America (UCA) in Managua, Nicaragua. It contains a monthly analysis of the Nicaraguan reality, analyses of Central American countries, articles on economic, ecological and social alternatives to neo-liberal economics, and debates on the new international situation. Subscriptions can be ordered via: *Revista Envío*, Apdo. Postal A-194, Managua, Nicaragua. envio@ns.uca.edu.ni Internet: http://www.uca.edu.ni/publications

Organizations and web sites

Alliance for Responsible Trade provides analysis of US trade policy in Latin America: www.art-us.org

Behind the Label provides multi-media information on anti-sweatshop campaigns: www.behindthelabel.org

Campaign for Labour Rights provides alerts on labour organizing, anti-sweatshop activism: www.summersault.com/~agj/clr

Comisión Económica para América Latina (CEPAL) provides information on economic development in Latin America and the Caribbean via studies on integration and trade, environment, foreign investment and other topics: www.eclac.cl and www.eclac.org

COMPARTE-RELACC emerges from the work of COMPARTE, a Chilean organization for fair trade which assists craft workers to establish channels of marketing which are fair and equitable. It has linked with RELACC in 2001: comparte@terra.cl

CONACADO RELACC of the Dominican Republic works with producers of cacao in the marketing of their product and is developing a wider network: conacado.inc@codetel.net.do

Coordinadora Regional de Investigaciones Económicos y Sociales (CRIES) conducts research on free trade agreements involving Central America and the Caribbean. www.cries.org/tlc

Council of Canadians programme on the Free Trade Area of the Americas and the Threat to Social Programmes, Environmental Sustainability and Social Justice in Canada and the Americas, contact Maude Barlow: www.canadians.org

El Observatorio Internacional, hosted by FUNDE in El Salvador, informs Central American civil society on the state of negotiations at the World Trade Organization as well as alternative activities: www.elobservatorio.org

Food and Agriculture Organization (FAO) provides information on trade and food security, international trade and food production, biotechnology, rural development, etc.: www.fao.org

Fundación para la Cooperación y el Desarrollo Comunal de El Salvador (CORDES) works in rural development via programmes in production, marketing and micro-enterprise in several departments of El Salvador. Its work in alternative marketing has focused on the promotion of farmers' markets and agro-industrial markets as well as coordinating with handicraft stores: cordes.ri@telesal.net

Hemispheric Social Alliance (HSA), known in Spanish as the Alianza Social Continental, is a network of labour organizations and citizens' coalitions representing more than 45 million people throughout the Americas. It was created to facilitate information exchange and create alternative proposals to build toward an alternative, democratic model of development: www.asc-hsa.org E-mail: asc@laneta.apc.org

Maquila Solidarity Network provides information and analysis on maquiladora workers: www.maquilasolidarity.org

Red Argentina de Comercio Comunitario (RACC) is an emerging network with the Red Global de Trueque (RGT) as a key experience. The RGT is an experience of the exchange of goods and services without the use of currency that has enjoyed widespread participation and impact in Argentina: rgt@egroups.com

Red Colombiana de Desarrollo y Comercialización Comunitaria (REDCOM) works with 32 groups, predominantly in southern Colombia, that are forming business associations of agricultural producers, agro-industrial efforts, crafts and community stores. They have also held 'mobile markets' (fairs): umata-pasto@yupimail.co

Red de Comercialización Comunitaria Alternativa (COMAL) of Honduras has programmes in market information, training, marketing of 'family basket' items and agricultural products, agro-industry and institutional strengthening: comal@bigfoot.com

Red de Intercambio y Comercio Alternativo de Abya Yala (RICAA) of California, USA works for sustainable development via the formation of a community-based network, the exchange of information, mutual support, and community programmes and services. An important foundation for RICAA is the Calpulli, a concrete way of forming a community based on cultural identity and history.

Red Ecuatoriana de Comercialización Comunitaria (REDECC) is hosted by RELACC and unites Ecuadoran organizations with ample experience in community marketing (RUNORSAL, UNORCFAV, MCCH, FEPP, CAMARI and RECCOSURE): relacc@uio.satnet.net

Red Internacional de Género y Comercio is an international network on trade and gender with participation from seven regions of the world: Africa, Asia, the Caribbean, Europe, Central and South America, North America and the Pacific. It works in research, the development of the network itself and of regional networks, and popular education. Its web site in Spanish is: www.laneta.apc.org

Red Latinoamericana de Comercialización Comunitaria (RELACC) is a corporation which consists of organizations belonging to national networks which practise community marketing in order to improve their standard of living and promote structural changes throughout Latin America. It currently represents 15 countries with central offices located in Quito, Ecuador: relacc@uio.satnet.net

Red Maya de Comercialización Comunitaria (REMACC) of Guatemala consists of organizations of small-scale producers and organized consumers in the marketing of basic grains and vegetables, institutional strengthening, community stores and exporting within Central America: remacc@terra.com.gt

Red Mexicana de Acción Frente al Libre Comercio (RMALC) is a citizen coalition which analyses, questions and influences economic and trade policy in Mexico: rmalc@laneta.apc.org Web site: www.rmalc.org.mx

Red Mexicana de Comercialización Comunitaria (REMECC) consists of 33 organizations which focus on community marketing efforts via direct marketing, the exchange of goods and services, community stores, organized bulk purchasing, rural–urban exchanges and the exportation of crafts: cedesa@laneta.apc.org

Red Nacional de Comercialización Comunitaria (RENACC) of Bolivia works with 70 organizations and 120 community-based groups in nine departments of the country, in the areas of crafts, agricultural products and training services: romeros@cosett.com.bo

Red Nicaragüense de Comercialización Comunitaria (RENICC) assists in linking small-scale producers with urban consumers via national and regional fairs throughout Nicaragua. There are 55 member organizations: renicc@teranet.com.ni

Red de Producción Orgánica y Comercialización Comunitaria (PROCOSOL) of Panama works with 19 member organizations to promote fairs which will link rural producers and urban consumers: rev@sinfo.net

RELACC Costa Rica is building its network in close coordination with the Frente Solidario of small-scale coffee-growers of Costa Rica. It has organized markets and fairs which promote urban and rural economic exchange.

RELACC Peru is a civil association which works in rural–urban product exchange. Its membership includes 18 groups of craft workers, 40 rural organizations and 3,000 *comedores populares* in Lima. It has held fairs to make products accessible to urban populations, has strengthened *comedores populares* via bulk purchases, and has an interest in developing responsible tourism: relaccpe@ec-red.com

7 Years After NAFTA, contact Alberto Arroyo, RMALC, Mexico.

United Students Against Sweatshops promotes student activism on US campuses: www.usasnet.org

Workers Rights Consortium, a student-initiated organization, analyses and monitors garment assembly factories: www.workersrights.org

ASIA *(Chapters 2, 4 and 10)*

Books

Mark Berger and Douglas Borer (eds.), *The Rise of East Asia*. London: Routledge, 1997. *(A critical look at economic development in East Asia.)*

Joseph Camilleri, Kamal Malhotra and Majid Tehranian, *Reimagining the Future: toward Democratic Governance*. La Trobe University, 2000. *(A set of proposals for restructuring global institutions, focusing on the international economic order, the UN and the security system.)*

Rebecca F. Catalla, *Socio-Cultural Vulnerability and Coping Strategies (SCVCS) Research Project, Reports 1–6*. AFSC, UNICEF and IDRC, 2000. *(These reports are available on-line from <go.to/scvcs>. A report of a two-year sociological study of vulnerable commu-*

nities in Cambodia – SCVCS Report No. 3, 'On the Edge of the Forest by the Side of the Road: People Dependent on Forest Resources in Koh Kong Province' – *provides detailed information about the struggles of the communities referred to in this book.)*

David Chandler, *A History of Cambodia*. Second edition. Boulder: Westview Press, 1992. *(The definitive source for contemporary Cambodian history.)*

Andre Dua and Daniel Esty, *Sustaining the Asia Pacific Miracle*. Institute for International Economics, 1997. *(Mainstream analysis of regional economic development with environmental focus.)*

Doug Guthrie, *Dragon in a Three-Piece Suit*. Princeton, Princeton University Press, 1999. *(A study of economic change at the firm level in China.)*

International Labour Organization, Task Force on Country Studies of Globalization, *Republic of Korea: Studies on the Social Dimensions of Globalization*. ILO, 1999. (Analysis of social impact of economic development in South Korea.)

Chalmers Johnson, Japan: *Who Governs? The Rise of the Developmental State*. Norton, 1995. *(A collection of essays that explores the differences between Japan's political economy and other economic arrangements.)*

Samuel Kim (ed.), *Korea's Globalization*. Cambridge: Cambridge University Press, 2000. *(A wide-ranging set of essays exploring different effects of globalization on South Korea, including the impact on migration, labour, gender, UN policy and security.)*

Ben Kiernan, *The Pol Pot Regime*. New Haven: Yale University Press, 1996. *(The definitive source on the Pol Pot period in Cambodia.)*

Sanitsuda Kochai, *Behind the Smile: Voices of Thailand*. Bangkok: Thai Development Support Committee, 1990.

Korea Economic Institute of America, *The Two Koreas in 2000: Sustaining Recovery and Seeking Reconciliation*. KEIA, 2000. *(A look at economic reform – the challenges and costs – in both South and North Korea.)*

Yayori Matsui, *Women in the New Asia*. London: Zed, 1999. *(An analysis of gender and economic development in Asia with an emphasis on grassroots responses to patriarchy and globalization.)*

Marcus Noland (ed.), *Economic Integration of the Korean Peninsula*. Institute for International Economics, 1998. *(A collection of essays that examines the relationship between North and South Korea in the light of current economic trends.)*

Nancy Lee Peluso, *Rich Forests, Poor People*. Berkeley: University of California Press, 1992. *(Describes the conflict for forest resources between communities and the state in Indonesia, examining both historical and contemporary materials.)*

Ansiur Rahman, *People's Self-Development: a Journey Through Experience*. London: Zed Books 1993. *(A personal exploration of the dynamics of community empowerment by one of the founders of participatory action research.)*

Vinod Raina et al. (eds.), *The Dispossessed*. ARENA Press, 1997. *(Country reports on ecological and industrial catastrophes in Asia.)*

Henry Rowen (ed.), *Behind East Asian Growth*. London: Routledge, 1998. *(A politically diverse set of essays that explores the rapid economic development of East Asian countries.)*

Sinith Sittirak, *The Daughters of Development: Women in a Changing Environment*. London: Zed Books, 1998. *(An exploration of gender and development with a focus on Thailand.)*

UN Development Programme, *China Human Development Report*. Beijing: UNDP, 1997. *(An analysis of the social impact of China's economic reform.)*

Willem van Kemenade, *China, Hong Kong, Taiwan, Inc.* Vintage, 1998. *(Mainstream analysis of Chinese economic reform and response to global economic trends.)*

Kosaku Yoshino (ed.), *Consuming Ethnicity and Nationalism: Asian Experiences*. University of Hawaii Press, 1999. *(A collection of essays that examines the impact of nationalism and ethnicity on political economy and globalization.)*

Organizations and web sites

Asia Monitor Resource Centre (AMRC)
(Tracks corporate conduct in Asia–Pacific; produces numerous reports.)
444–446 Nathan Road, 8-B Kowloon, Hong Kong.
Phone: 852-2332-1346. Fax: 852-2385-5319.
admin@amrc.org.hk
http://home.pacific.net.hk/~amrc

Asian Regional Exchange for New Alternatives (ARENA)
(Progressive thinktank; produces books and reports.)
Flat 6, 13th Floor, Block A, Fuk Keung Industrial Building,
66-68 Tong Mi Road, Kowloon, Hong Kong.
Phone: 852-2805-6193, 2805-6270. Fax: 852-2504-2986.
arena@asianexchange.org
http://www.asianexchange.org

Cambodia Development Resource Institute
(One of the foremost sources of independent information on social
and economic development in Cambodia.)
www.cdri.org.kh

Committee on Asian Women (CAW)
(Produces materials on women and globalization in the region.)
386/60 Soi Ratchadaphisek 42, Ratchadaphisek Rd., Ladyao
Bangkok, Chatujak 10900 Thailand.
Phone: 662-930-5634. Fax: 930-5633.
caw@mozart.inet.co.th
http://caw.jinbo.net

Development Alternatives with Women for a New Era (DAWN)
(Activist-oriented network that focuses on gender and economic development.)
DAWN Secretariat, The University of the South Pacific, Suva, Fiji.
Phone/Fax: (679) 314 770.
dawn@is.com.fj
http://www.dawn.org.fj/index.html

Focus on the Global South (FOCUS)
(Progressive thinktank; specializes in trade issues and global economic institutions.)
    c/o CUSRI, Chulalongkorn University, Bangkok 10330 Thailand.
    Phone: 662 218 7363/7364/7365. Fax: 662 255 9976.
    http://www.focusweb.org

Global Village
(Fair trade organization in Japan.)
    2-16-29-2F Jiyugaoka
    Meguro-ku, Tokyo, Japan
    Phone: 81-3-5731-8871. Fax: 81-3-5731-6677.
    gv@gn.apc.org
    http://www.globalvillage.or.jp/

Hong Kong Christian Industrial Committee (HKCIC)
(Focuses on corporate conduct and labour organizing.)
    57 Peking Road, 7/F, Kowloon, Hong Kong.
    Phone: 852-2366-5860. Fax: 852-2724-5098.
    hkcic@hknet.com
    http://www.cic.org.hk

Hong Kong Women Workers' Association
(Focuses on organizing among women workers.)
    Tsui Ping South Estate, Tsui Ying House G/F 1-3A, Kwun Tong,
    Kowloon, Hong Kong.
    Phone: 852-27904848. Fax: 27904922.
    hkwwa@pacific.net.hk

International Federation of Alternative Trade (IFAT)
(Directory of members in Asia-Pacific region.)
    http://www.peoplelink.org/ifat/

Japan Committee for Negros Campaign
(Focuses on solidarity between Japan and Negros, Philippines.)
    Sunrise Building 3F, 2-4-15 Ohkubo, Shinjuku-ku, Tokyo, Japan.
    Phone: 81-3-5273-8860. Fax: 81-3-5273-8667.
    http://www.jca.apc.org/jcnc/

Korean Confederation of Trade Unions (KCTU)
(One of the most active trade unions in the region.)
    5th Daeyoung Building, 139 Youngdeungpo-2-ga, Youngdeungpo-ku,
    Seoul 150-032 Korea.
    Phone: +82-2-2636-0165. Fax.: +82-2-2635-1134.
    inter@kctu.org
    http://kctu.org/english/

Korean Women Workers Associations United
(Advocacy group focusing on organizing women workers.)
> Room 1305-6 13th Floor, Korean Ecumenical Building,
> 136–56 Yonji-dong, Jongno-ku, Seoul 110-470 Korea.
> Phone: 82-2-708-4826. Fax: 82-2-708-4622.
> kwwa@chollian.net

NGO Forum on Cambodia
(The umbrella group of Cambodian and international NGOs working together on advocacy issues. From their web site links are available to a wealth of resources, bibliographies and articles.)
> admin@ngo.forum.org.kh
> www.bigpond.com.kh/users/ngoforum

Pacific–Asia Resource Centre (PARC)
(Tracks issues of globalization, particularly the impact of Japanese corporations.)
> 2F Toyo Building 1-7-11 Kanda Awaji-cho Chiyoda-ku,
> Tokyo 101-0063 Japan.
> Phone: 81-3-5209-3455. Fax: 81-3-5209-3453.
> parc@jca.apc.org
> http://www.jca.apc.org/parc/

People's Plan Study Group
(Activist group with interest in impact of globalization on region.)
> Okubo 2-4-15-3,. Shinjuku-ku, Tokyo 169-0072 Japan.
> Phone/Fax: 81-3-5273-8362.
> ppsg@jca.apc.org

People's Solidarity for Participatory Democracy (PSPD)
(Korean civic movement working on economic corruption and greater democracy.)
> 3F Anguk Building 175-3, Anguk-Dong Chongno-Gu,
> Seoul 110-240 Korea.
> Phone: 82-2-723-4250. Fax: 82-2-723-5055.
> pspdint@pspd.org
> http://www.pspd.org

Rural Women Knowing All
(Organization and magazine devoted to needs of rural women in China.)
> 103 Dianmenxi Dajie, Dajie, Beijing 100009 People's Republic of China.
> Phone: 86-10-66164191. Fax: 86-10-62354474.

Third World Network
(Specializes in international economic issues and progressive alternatives.)
> 228 Macalister Road, 10400 Penang, Malaysia.
> Phone: 60-4-2266728/2266159. Fax: 60-4-2264505.
> twn@igc.apc.org
> http://www.twnside.org.sg/

Publications

Asian Exchange. Occasional publication of the Asian Regional Exchange for New Alternatives (ARENA). One recent issue examined popular responses to the Asian financial crisis, with a section on economic alternatives. For more information: arena@asianexchange.org

Asian Labour Update. Put out by the Asia Monitor Resource Centre. Subscriptions $20 a year. Contact: eds@amrc.org.hk.

Asian Perspective, Vol. 23, No. 4 (1999): special issue on Asia and globalization.

Asia Solidarity Quarterly. Joint effort of People's Solidarity for Participatory Democracy (PSPD) and the Resource Centre for Asian NGOs at Sungkonghoe University in Seoul. Subscriptions $50 a year. Contact Youngmi Yang at pspdint@pspd.org or visit the web site at http://www.pspd.org

Change. Hong Kong Christian Industrial Committee newsletter. For more information: http://www.cic.org.hk

China Labour Bulletin. For more information: http://www.china-labour.org.hk

Civil Society. Publication of the Citizens' Coalition for Economic Justice, one of Korea's oldest NGOs. Subscriptions $30 a year. Contact Sister Rose Guercio at mmm@ccej.or.kr

Focus on Trade. Electronic journal of Focus on the Global South. To subscribe or to order any of their other publications, visit their web site at http://www.focusweb.org

Foreign Policy in Focus publishes briefs on US foreign policy. To view their publications on US policy in Asia, go to:
http://www.foreignpolicy-infocus.org/indices/regions/asia.html

Working Women is the publication of the Korean Women Workers' Associations United. Annual subscriptions $20 for Asian countries and $30 for all others. Send cheques or postal orders to KWWAU at 1st floor, 337-4 Ahyeon 2-dong, Mapo-gu, Seoul 121-859 Korea.

EUROPE *(Chapters 7 and 9)*

Books and Reports

The Crucible Group, *Seeding Solutions, Policy Options for Genetic Resources.* Ottawa: International Development Research Centre, 2001.

Graham Dutfield, *Intellectual Property Rights, Trade and Biodiversity.* London: Earthscan Publications, 2000.

Dan Leskien and Michael Flitner, *Intellectual Property Rights, Plant Genetic Resources: Options for a Sui Generis System.* Rome: IPGRI, 1997.

Gurdial Singh Nijar, 'In Defence of Local Community Knowledge and Biodiversity: a Conceptual Framework and the Essential Elements of a Rights Regime'. Third World Network, Paper 1, 1996.

Geoff Tansey, *Trade, Intellectual Property, Food and Biodiversity: Key Issues and Options for the 1999 Review of Article 27.3(b) of the TRIPS Agreement.* London: Quaker Peace and Service, 1999. Available at the Quaker United Nations Office, Geneva (web page: www.quno.org).

Organizations and web sites

Alternative Information Network. Network of independent journalists in the Balkans with coverage of regional and local events in regional languages as well as English. http://www.aimpress.ch/index.htm

Food and Agriculture Organization. United Nations agency dedicated to raising nutrition and food production standards and rural conditions. Information available on urban gardening. http://www.fao.org/

Genetic Resources Action International (Grain). www.grain.org

Institute for Agricultural Trade Policy. www.iatp.org

International Centre for Trade and Sustainable Development. www.ictsd.org

International Crisis Group. Think-tank established after the tragedies of Bosnia-Herzegovina and Rwanda to report on events in countries facing potential conflict. Many reports on Bosnia-Herzegovina. http://www.crisisweb.org/

International Food Policy Research Institute. Research organization dedicated to identifying policies for meeting the food needs of developing countries. Information available on urban food production. http://www.ifpri.org/

International Plant Genetic Resources Institute. www.cgiar..org/ipgri

Office of the High Representative. The international authority established by the Dayton Accords to oversee governmental affairs in Bosnia-Herzegovina. http://www.ohr.int/

Organization for Security and Cooperation in Europe (OSCE). Works on democratization, human rights, elections, arms control and security-building measures in Bosnia-Herzegovina. http://www.oscebih.org/languages.asp

Radio Free Europe. Daily and archived news from throughout the region. http://www.rferl.org/

United Nations Mission in Bosnia and Herzegovina. Provides international police and civil affairs assistance. http://www.unmibh.org/

World Trade Organization. www.wto.org

Index

accountability 125

activism, for civil rights 43; community 114; consumer-based 51; against dams 15; for debt relief 15, 65-72; against deforestation 15, 142-3; environmental 15, 142-3; against genetically modified food 15; and the Internet 45, 51; on labour issues 15, 37-52, 74-83; against the Multilateral Agreement on Investment 15; and networking 18, 45, 47, 65-6, 125, 142-3; for peace 41; in the South 65; and street theatre 46, 50; student 49; against sweatshops 17, 37-52; in Washington (2000) 46; at the WTO (1999) 1, 46, 66

advertising 39, 50, 139

AFL/CIO 48, 80

Africa 3, 11, 13, 49, 65-72, 120, 129; East 65-72; southern 65

Agailhjara 132-3

agriculture, agro-forestry 32-3; agro-industry 36, 101-2, 109; cooperative 101-3, 109, 134; and credit 61, 69, 72, 101-3; diversity in 33, 88, 90-1, 94, 97, 101, 103; export 26, 69, 120; and fair trade products 129-35; and globalization 97, 100, 138; industrial 23, 90, 94, 101; integrated 141; and network marketing 108-12, 129; organic 109, 123-4, 129, 131-2, 134, 136-9; services 69; slash-and-burn 28; small 69, 97, 99-105, 108-9, 111-12, 144; and structural adjustment 69; subsistence 17-18, 31, 69, 100; training in 31-3; urban 120-5

aid 24-5, 72, 114, 120, 129, 134, 143

AIDS 69-70, 85

Alaska 41

Alternative Livelihood Award 139

Alternative Trade Japan 131

American Federation of State, County and Municipal Employees 46

American Friends Service Committee (AFSC) vii, 17, 30-5, 39, 41, 46-7, 52, 76, 78, 80, 100, 104, 114, 116, 125

Americas 3, 13, 45

Andean Community Common System on Access to Genetic Resources 88-9

Andean Pact 88-9

Andes 17

Arab peoples 2

Argentina 1

Asahi Shimbum 133